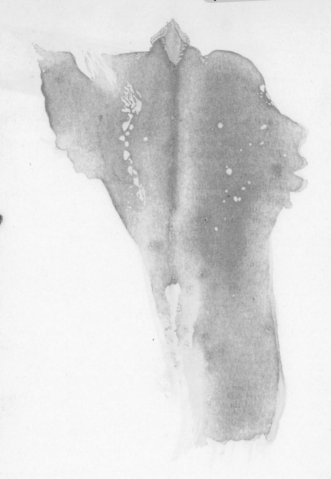

BELLS ARE RINGING

Bells are Ringing

Book and Lyrics by
BETTY COMDEN
and
ADOLPH GREEN

Music by
JULE STYNE

Random House
New York

BELLS ARE RINGING *was first presented by The Theatre Guild
at the Sam S. Shubert Theatre, New York City, on November
29, 1956, with the following cast:*

(In Order of Appearance)

SUE SUMMERS	Jean Stapleton
GWYNNE SMITH	Pat Wilkes
ELLA PETERSON	Judy Holliday
CARL	Peter Gennaro
INSPECTOR BARNES	Dort Clark
FRANCIS	Jack Weston
SANDOR	Eddie Lawrence
JEFF MOSS	Sydney Chaplin
LARRY HASTINGS	George S. Irving
TELEPHONE MAN	Eddie Heim
LUDWIG SMILEY	Frank Milton
CHARLES BESSEMER	Frank Green
DR. KITCHELL	Bernie West
BLAKE BARTON	Frank Aletter
ANOTHER ACTOR	Frank Green
CLERK	Tom O'Steen
OLGA	Norma Doggett
HENCHMAN FROM CORVELLO MOB	John Perkins
OTHER HENCHMAN	Kasimir Kokich
CAROL	Ellen Ray
PAUL ARNOLD	Steve Roland
MICHELLE	Michelle Reiner
MASTER OF CEREMONIES	Eddie Heim
SINGER AT NIGHTCLUB	Frank Green

WAITER	Ed Thompson
MAITRE D'HOTEL	David McDaniel
POLICE OFFICER	Gordon Woodburn
MADAME GRIMALDI	Donna Sanders
MRS. MALLET	Jeannine Masterson

DANCERS

GIRLS: Norma Doggett, Phyllis Dorne, Patti Karr, Barbara Newman, Nancy Perkins, Marsha Rivers, Beryl Towbin, Anne Wallace.

BOYS: Doria Avila, Frank Derbas, Don Emmons, Eddie Heim, Kasimir Kokich, Tom O'Steen, Willy Summer, Ben Vargas, Billy Wilson.

SINGERS

GIRLS: Pam Abbott, Joanne Birks, Urylee Leonardos, Jeannine Masterson, Michelle Reiner, Donna Sanders.

BOYS: Frank Green, Marc Leon, David McDaniel, Paul Michael, Julian Patrick, Steve Roland, Ed Thompson, Gordon Woodburn.

SCENES

ACT ONE

ACT TWO

MUSICAL NUMBERS

ACT ONE

Opening	Bells Are Ringing	Girls
Scene 1	It's a Perfect Relationship	Ella
Scene 2	On My Own	Jeff and Ensemble
	You've Got to Do It	Jeff
Scene 3	It's a Simple Little System	Sandor and Ensemble
Scene 5	Is It a Crime?	Ella
Scene 8	Hello, Hello There!	Ella, Jeff and Ensemble
Scene 9	I Met a Girl	Jeff and Ensemble
Scene 15	Long Before I Knew You	Ella and Jeff

ACT TWO

Scene 1	Mu-cha-cha	Ella and Carl
	Dance	Carol, Carl and Dancing Ensemble
Scene 2	Just in Time	Jeff, Ella and Ensemble
Scene 3	Drop That Name	Ella and Ensemble
	The Party's Over	Ella
Scene 4	Salzburg	Sue and Sandor
Scene 5	The Midas Touch	Singer, Boys and Girls
Scene 6	Reprise: Long Before I knew You	Jeff
Scene 7	I'm Goin' Back	Ella
	Finale	The Company

Entire production directed by Jerome Robbins

Sets and costumes designed by Raoul Pene du Bois

Dances and musical numbers staged by Jerome Robbins

Musical direction by Milton Rosenstock

Orchestrations by Robert Russell Bennett

Vocal arrangements and direction by Herbert Greene *and* Buster Davis

Dance arrangements and incidental scoring by John Morris

Lighting by Peggy Clark

BELLS ARE RINGING

ACT ONE

ACT ONE

Susanswerphone Advertisement
At rise, eight GIRLS, *looking lonely and disconsolate, are seen on stage.*

OFF-STAGE ANNOUNCER
(*With unctuous concern*)
Ladies and gentlemen, has this ever happened to you? These girls missed an important telephone call.
(GIRLS *sigh, then they sing*)
All around there's the sound of the midsummer night;
Bells in the air are ringing everywhere.
I can hear footsteps that pass on the street
And lovers rushing to meet.
Here alone I can only imagine the sight—
Me on the town in some bewitching gown—
But I just wait at the end of the line
As bells are ringing; the bells keep ringing—
Oh why, oh why can't the next call be mine?

OFF-STAGE ANNOUNCER
A sad story, girls—(*They nod sadly*) But it need not have happened. (*They look up hopefully*) Perhaps—during the time you were out—*he* called ("*Ohhhh*" *from the* GIRLS) but no one was there to answer your telephone. (GIRLS *slump despondently,*

3

sighing, "Ohhhh!") Don't let the same thing happen tomorrow night!

GIRLS

(*Sing-song*)

But what can we do?

OFF-STAGE ANNOUNCER

Subscribe to an answering service. Use Susanswerphone!

GIRLS

Susanswerphone?

OFF-STAGE ANNOUNCER

Yes. It gives and takes your messages as it does for business executives, doctors, and theatre celebrities on New York's smart East Side. Now, this is what can happen when you subscribe to Susanswerphone.

(*Sound of phone ringing.*)

GIRLS

(*Picking up imaginary phones*)

Hello?

OPERATOR'S VOICE

This is your answering service.

GIRLS

Yes?

OPERATOR'S VOICE

While you were out the agency called. You got the job!

4

GIRLS
(*Thrilled*)

Oh!

OPERATOR'S VOICE
And your lawyer called. Your uncle left you all his money in his will!

GIRLS
(*More thrilled*)

Oh!!!

OPERATOR'S VOICE
And *he* called and I gave him your message, so he's waiting for you right now!!

GIRLS
(*Most thrilled*)

Oh!!!!
(*They sing*)
Thank you Susanswerphone!!
(*They dash off joyously. One can only feel that a full, happy life is spreading before them.*)

OFF-STAGE ANNOUNCER
Ring us up at our sumptuous, luxurious offices where our vast personnel of well-trained girls are ready even now to serve you! Susanswerphone!!
(*While he is still speaking, against a musical background of celestial harps,*

The Lights Fade

SCENE 1

The Susanswerphone office. A hot New York summer day, late afternoon. A small squalid room down a few steps from street level, with barely any light coming in through one dirty window which looks out on a hall. An old chair is on one side, with springs caved in and stuffings coming out. The place is littered with old coffee containers, filled ash trays, empty Coke bottles, movie magazines and bedroom slippers. A door, stage left, leads to the bathroom, which the girls use to change clothes.

In the center of the crowded, cluttered room is a telephone switchboard. The desk in front of the board is covered with message pads, a file, phone books, etc.

Seated at the switchboard, wearing a smock, is SUE SUMMERS, *plain and fortyish, owner of Susanswerphone. Her manner on the phone is always cool and impersonal. In the chair sits* GWYNNE SMITH, *one of her two answering service girls, reading a magazine.* GWYNNE *is plump, sedentary.*

SUE

(On phone)

Yes, Mr. Townsend. Your broker called. That is all. *(She disconnects, tears up the message briskly and drops it in the waste-basket. The phone rings. She picks up)*

La Petite Bergère French Restaurant.

> *(She says this in a terrible American accent: La Pateet Burjer.)*

6

WOMAN'S VOICE

I'd like to—

SUE

We're closed for all of August. (*She disconnects. Ring*)
Susanswerphone.

GIRL'S VOICE

(*Gushing with happiness*)
This is Miss Stevens—

SUE

Yes, Miss Stevens. No messages.

GIRL'S VOICE

Oh—you must be the other one. Where is—?

SUE

(*Annoyed*)
She'll be on later, Miss Stevens.

GIRL'S VOICE

I just wanted to tell you . . . Mr. Humboldt and I are getting
married— (*Giggles*) So from now on we'll have *one* account
with you together—instead of two.

SUE

Oh. Well—congratulations. (*She unplugs, looks stricken*)
Oh!

GWYNNE

(*Barely looking up from her reading*)
What happened, Sue?

SUE

We just lost an account. I bet Ella had something to do with this. Ella!

ELLA

(*Off stage*)
I'm just cleaning the canary's cage. Be right in!

SUE

(*Calling to her*)
Ella! Miss Number 63 and Mr. Number 78 are getting married—!

ELLA

(*Running in excitedly with the bird cage. She is blond, pretty —with a quick mind and vivid imagination that helps her improvise in any situation. Warm and sympathetic, she loves her job and regards her subscribers as personal friends though, of course, she has never met them*)

Ohhh, good! When did it happen?!!

SUE

(*Suspiciously*)
Ella, did you—?

ELLA

(*Suddenly defensive, then with great innocence*)
I had nothing to do with it. I just happened to know that Miss Number 63 wanted to mate her female Siamese cat and I also knew that Mr. Number 78 had a male Siamese cat—so I told her and she called him—and they *all* got together.

SUE

(*Shaking her head*)

My cuckoo cousin! (*Getting up*) Take over the board, please
—but remember—an answering service is not the Department
of Welfare! (*She starts putting things on as* ELLA *sits at board*)
I've told you a thousand times—you're too darn friendly with
the subscribers. (ELLA *starts nodding her head in rhythm with
this oft-heard speech and mouthing the words with her*) Just
give and take messages—that's all. I'll be back later. (*She starts
out, sticks head back through the window*) I'm warning you,
Ella—watch it!

(*She is gone. The phone rings.*)

ELLA

(*Her phone manner is always warm and personal. More than
that, she actually assumes a different character for each subscriber, and throws herself into these continually, with an
effortless abandon. At this moment she answers the phone with
a flawless French accent*)

La Petite Bergère Restaurant Français. *Bonjour!*

MAN'S VOICE

I should like to make a reservation for—

ELLA

I am sorree, we are closed for all of Auguste.

MAN'S VOICE

Thank you.

9

ELLA

De rien! (*Unplugs. Ring*) Susanswerphone.

MRS. MALLET'S VOICE

Hello. This is Mrs. Mallet. Is this Santa Claus?

ELLA

Yes, Mrs. Mallet. Put Jimmy on.

JIMMY

(*Child's voice*)

Hello, Santa Claus.

ELLA

(*Assumes booming Santa voice*)

Ho, ho, ho! Jimmy! I hear you won't eat your spinach again. That makes Santa very sad. Ho! Ho! Ho!

JIMMY

Ohhh—all right, Santa Claus. I will. Good-bye.

ELLA

Good-bye. (*Unplugs. Ring*) Susanswerphone.

MADAME GRIMALDI'S VOICE

(*Rich and operatic*)

Hello! This is Rosina Grimaldi!

ELLA

Oh, how's your laryngitis?

MADAME GRIMALDI'S VOICE

(*Executes a coloratura trill.* ELLA *looks delighted and holds headpiece away from her so* GWYNNE *can hear*)
And I owe it all to you and your wonderful mustard plaster!

ELLA

Oh, I'm so glad! And listen—that mustard plaster is so pure, if there's any left over, you can put it on a hot dog.

MADAME GRIMALDI'S VOICE

I'm very grateful! I'm sending you beautiful ball gown made for *Traviata!*

ELLA

Oh, you mustn't! (*Click.* ELLA *unplugs, excitedly*) Hey, Madame Grimaldi's sending me a ball gown made for *Traviata.* (*Pause—suddenly disconsolate*) When will I ever wear it?

GWYNNE

You could put it on every time Jeffrey Moss calls.

ELLA

(*Innocently*)

Jeffrey Moss?

GWYNNE

Oh, come on. You melt every time you hear his voice.

ELLA

I don't know what you're talking about. I wonder what he looks like?

THE BELLS ARE RINGING

(*Ring.* ELLA *sits on a stool at the side of the switchboard, plugs in.*)

GWYNNE

Well, let's see—about eighty years old, long furry tail—

ELLA

Jeffrey Moss residence.

OLGA'S VOICE

(*A whining screech*)
Can I talk to Jeffrey, please?

ELLA

(*With a weary, resigned look at* GWYNNE, *indicating "it's that one again"*)
Who's calling?

OLGA'S VOICE

You know who's calling! It's Olga! I've called four times already. I've been waiting since eleven for him to take me to the *races*. I can't wait around all day for him to take me to the *races*—for heavens *sake!*
(*Click.* ELLA *disconnects.*)

ELLA

(*Rising—mimicking* OLGA'S VOICE)
The *races!* That's all he needs is to be taken to the *races!* As if he hasn't got enough trouble as it is!

GWYNNE

Why don't you stop worrying about that playboy!

ELLA

He's not a playboy! He's a very talented writer.

GWYNNE

Yeah—but all he does is play— He never writes.

ELLA

He's only been doing that since his partner left him—He's afraid to write alone. You don't know him the way I do— He's sensitive—he's intelligent—he's—I wonder what he looks like—

GWYNNE

(*Removing her smock*)

Look—the Sleeping Prince is Number 37 on the board— Remember? He's just Plaza O-double four double three.

ELLA

Oh, Gwynne, he doesn't mean any more to me than any other subscriber—(*Alarm clock sounds. She rushes to turn it off*) Six-thirty! I've got to wake him again. He checked in at seven this morning, as usual, and I've been calling him since two.

(*She sits at the board and applies fresh lipstick.*)

GWYNNE

(*Watching all this*)

Yeah.

CARL

(*The delivery boy from the drug store enters with an order as ELLA dials*)

Hi, girls. Mind if I take the short cut?

ELLA

Sure, Carl—go ahead.

> (CARL *crosses in front of the switch board, and exits.* GWYNNE *pours coffee for* ELLA *and places it on the switchboard.*)

JEFF'S VOICE

> (*A hoarse, gravelly groan that seems to issue from some Stygian cave forlorn*)

Uhhhhhhhh.

ELLA

> (*Using little old lady's voice*)

Hello, Mr. Moss.

JEFF'S VOICE

> (*Feebly conscious*)

Oh, is that you, Mom?

ELLA

It's six-thirty—time to get up. Your producer, Mr. Hastings, called, and I have another message for you. Just a minute—
(*She looks through messages.*)

GWYNNE

Aren't you ever going to give up that old lady's voice you use with him?

ELLA

> (*Flatly*)

He needs a mother. (GWYNNE *shakes her head, picks up her purse and exits with a farewell gesture*) Mr. Moss? You asked me to repeat this message to you: "Get up, you gin-soaked idiot, and write your play, *The Midas Touch*."

Beautiful prose. Tell you what, Mom—call me back in a coupla hours.

ELLA

Oh, no, Mr. Moss . . .

>   (*She sings a few notes of "Reveille" in a coy, sunny little soprano.* JEFF'S VOICE *counters with a weary rendition of "Taps" that fades away in sleep as he hangs up. She resets the alarm with a sad smile, then sings*)

It's crazy—it's ridiculous—it doesn't make sense,
That's true—
But what can I do?

I'm in love
With a man—
Plaza O-double four, double three—
It's a perfect relationship—
I can't see him—He can't see me.
I'm in love
With a voice—
Plaza O-double four, double three—
What a perfect relationship—
I talk to him and he just talks to me.

And yet I can't help wond'ring
What does he look like?
I wish I knew!
What does he look like?
Is he six-foot-seven or three-foot-two?
Has he eyes of brown or baby blue?
Big and mighty or underfed?

Trim black mustache or beard of red?
Can he dance like Fred Astaire?
Is he dark or is he fair?
Pompadour or not a hair?
Well, I don't care!

I'm in love
With a man—
Plaza O-double four, double three—
What a perfect relationship—
And that's how things should always be.
Our love can never lose it's mystery,
'Cause I'll never meet him and he'll never meet me.
No, he'll never meet me.

What does he look like?
My Sleeping Prince?
What does he look like?
He could be the fat and balding type,
Or rugged tweeds and briar pipe,
Dark-rimmed glasses—super-mind—
Or the sweet, poetic kind.
It doesn't matter what he'd be—
How he'd love me!

    (*A ring interrupts and brings* ELLA *back to reality*)
Susanswerphone.

JEFF'S VOICE

Hello. Mom? If Olga calls again, stall her for me, will you?

ELLA
(*Mom's voice*)

Yes, Mr. Moss.

JEFF'S VOICE

That's a good old Mom.

ELLA

(*Very let-down*)

Yes, Mr. Moss.
(*He hangs up. She unplugs, shaken out of her dream,
then sings*)
He's still just a voice—
Plaza O-double four, double three—
What a perfect relationship—
I can't see him—He can't see me.
He calls me Mom; he thinks I'm sixty-three—
And I'll never meet him and he'll never meet me.
No, he'll never meet me.
(*She flops down resignedly into the armchair. Two men,*
BARNES *and* FRANCIS, *enter. They "case" the room quickly.*
ELLA *turns to them*)
Hello.

BARNES

(*Elaborately polite*)

Uh—how do you do! My name is Barnes.

ELLA

Yes, Mr. Barnes?

BARNES

We're doing some—uh—research on answering services—for
—uh—(*He seems to have forgotten his lines and turns to*
FRANCIS, *who mouths* Fortune) Fortune Magazine. We'd like
to ask you a couple of questions?

17

ELLA

(*Excited and flattered*)

Oh, of course! Please make yourselves at home! I'm having coffee—I'll wash out some more cups.

BARNES

(*Watches her exit into bathroom*)

Thanks. Thank you very much. (*As soon as she is out, his manner changes abruptly. He is an aggressive, not overly bright detective.* FRANCIS *is his timid, sensible assistant*) Francis, the minute she gets on the phone, turn on that tape recorder.

FRANCIS

Are you sure about this, Inspector Barnes?

BARNES

Mr. Barnes, you meathead! I'm going to get a promotion for closing this joint.

FRANCIS

But just because the law arrests all those girls at "All-Alone—A-Phone," doesn't mean every answering service is a front for a—"lonely hearts club." She seems like such a nice girl—

(BARNES *silences him as* ELLA *enters with cups.*)

ELLA

Well—now, what can I tell you?

BARNES

(*With a coarse grin as he looks her up and down*)

Well, let's see— Tell me—how do you like your work?

ELLA

(*Open and chatty as she pours and serves the coffee*)

Oh, I love it here! I used to be just a plain switchboard operator—in a lingerie house— Pretty dull except for a little modeling on the side.

BARNES

(*Leering*)

Modeling on the side, huh?

ELLA

But here it's all so personal. I talk to so many different kinds of people—and can give each one the particular kind of help he needs. My cousin Sue thinks I spend too much time on each one. She says, "Get it over with fast and get on to the next!"

BARNES

(*Exchanging look with* FRANCIS)

Yes, of course.
       (*Ring.*)

ELLA

Oh, excuse me. (*She goes behind the board and plugs in.* FRANCIS *places a small tape recorder on top of the switchboard*) Madame Grimaldi's.

BARITONE VOICE

Ees Madame at home?

ELLA

No, the Madame is out.
       (*They are listening intently.*)

19

BARITONE VOICE

Are you her answering service girl?

ELLA

There are several of us. Which girl do you want?

BARITONE VOICE

The mustard plaster one.

ELLA

(*Pleased*)

Oh, that's me.

BARITONE VOICE

Madame Grimaldi raved so—could you give me the formula —and how much do you charge?

ELLA

Charge? Oh, for any friend of Madame Grimaldi's, it's free!

BARNES

(*Grabbing her*)

Okay, sister! Hang up!

ELLA

Oh, excuse me. I'm sorry, sir. Good-bye. (*Hangs up and turns to* BARNES, *who has pulled her out of her chair*) What *is* this?

BARNES

Get your toothbrush and come along.

ELLA

My toothbrush?

GWYNNE
(*Coming in*)

What's going on here?

BARNES

What do *you* do?

GWYNNE
(*Scared*)

I work here.

BARNES
(*Grabbing her*)

Maybe you better come along, too.

SUE
(*Entering*)

Why, girls, what are these men doing here?

BARNES

Who's *she?*

SUE
(*Angrily*)

I happen to own this place—that's "who's she." What do *you* want?

BARNES
(*Revealing badge with satisfaction*)

We're closing up this joint. You're all coming along. Women's Detention Home—Inspector Barnes, Vice Squad!

SUE

(*Gasping, almost fainting, to* ELLA)
I knew it! I knew you'd get us in trouble! I warned you!

ELLA

(*Completely baffled*)
But, Inspector! What did we do wrong?

BARNES

(*Terribly pleased with himself*)
I'll just let you speak for yourself.
(*Turns on tape recorder and they all listen.*)

ELLA'S VOICE

"Madame Grimaldi's. No, the Madame is out. Which girl
do you want? There are several of us. Oh, that's me! Charge?
Oh, for any friend of Madame Grimaldi's, it's free!"
(ELLA *reacts with that look of surprised and approving
enjoyment at hearing one's own voice played back.*)

BARNES

(*Moving in for the kill*)
Now, which one of you is the Madam?

ELLA

(*Starting to explain reasonably*)
That's Madame Rosina Grimaldi, the opera star, and I
happened to recommend a mustard plaster to her for a cold, and
this friend of hers—Ohhhh! (*With sudden realization*) Have
you got a *dirty* mind! (*Very strongly, angry now*) Okay,
Inspector, you take me down to the Women's Detention Home!

Before I get through with you, I'll have you demoted to a chicken inspector!

SUE

(*Witheringly*)
And here's our list of subscribers, Inspector!
(*She hands him the list.*)

BARNES

(*Looking at it—dejected*)
All right! I made a mistake—

ELLA

Ha!
(*She goes to sit at the board.*)

BARNES

Maybe.

FRANCIS

(*Shaking his head*)
Always in such a hurry to uncover a crime. I keep telling him—get the evidence like all the others do.

BARNES

(*Furious*)
Shut up!
(*A face appears at the window.*)

SANDOR

(*Through the window*)
Liebchen!

SUE

(*Flustered and excited*)

Sandor!

SANDOR

(*Entering. He is seedy, but suavely Mittel-European. He speaks with a Continental accent, and has the silky charm of the professional con man*)

Ah! My dear Sue! I—

BARNES

Who's that?

SUE

(*Showing him off proudly*)

This is my new partner! Sandor, this is Inspector Barnes.

ELLA

(*Astonished*)

Partner!

SUE

And this is the staff—Gwynne Smith and my cousin, Ella Peterson.

SANDOR

(*Smoothly, as* SUE *watches him adoringly*)

Charmed! Allow me to present myself—J. Sandor Prantz, President of the Titanic Record Company—purveyors of classical music—Titanic Records, the highest fi of them all! This lovely lady has persuaded me to move my recording enterprises here and join forces with Susanswerphone to expedite a wide expansion program on an over-all top urban saturation basis.

BARNES

(*Taken in by him*)

Uh-huh! Uh-huh! Well, Professor, she'll tell you what's been going on here. (*To* ELLA) I'll be around—and I'll be listening in.

ELLA

Monitoring the phones?

BARNES

Any personal or friendly talk or direct contact, little lady, and I close this joint—but quick! Come on, Francie!
(*He exits.*)

FRANCIS

(*Sympathetically*)

Please take care, miss. You know, it's illegal to pass on information you receive to subscribers—even for a mustard plaster—

BARNES

(*Off stage*)

FRANCIE!
(FRANCIS *exits, exchanging an understanding wave of the fingers with* ELLA.)

SUE

Oh, Sandor, when I came in the Inspector was about to take us all to the Women's Detention Home.
(*Ring.* ELLA *plugs in.*)

ELLA

Kramer Music.

VOICE

Message for Kramer. This is Morty Hopper of the Pyramid Club. We need some songs fast, so Friday, 10 A.M., we're gonna have a lotta song writers in to peddle their fish. Got that?

ELLA

(*Writing*)

Ten A.M., Friday, Pyramid Club—song writers' auditions. Thank you. (*Disconnects, then starts dialing happily*) Hey, what an opportunity for Dr. Kitchell! I tell him about it; he takes his songs over there—and—

ALL

ELLA!

ELLA

(*Unplugging—very much upset*)

But if he could only sell one song it might change his whole life.

SUE

All right! What business is that of yours? Dr. Kitchell is a dentist and he'd rather be a song writer.

SANDOR

Now, Sue, don't upset yourself. Sandor is here. He will look after things. Well—*Aufwiedersehen*.

(*He starts to leave.*)

SUE

Oh, Sandor—aren't you taking me to dinner?

SANDOR

My dear Sue—I am desolate, but I must go to an important board of directors meeting of Titanic Records—and tell them of our new million dollar expansion program for Susanswerphone. Oh, by the way, I seem to have nothing but twenty's and fifty's with me. Do you have a couple of singles to spare? You know these cab drivers.

SUE

(*Takes some money from her purse and hands it to him*)
Here you are, Sandor.

SANDOR

(*Kissing her hand*)
Thank you, *Liebchen!* Good night, girls! *Aufwiedersehen!*
(*He exits. Ring.*)

ELLA

Susanswerphone.

HASTING'S VOICE

(*Angry and disturbed*)
This is Larry Hastings calling. Any messages? Jeff Moss call?

ELLA

No, but Blake Barton, the actor, called. Wanted to know if there's a part for him in your new production, *The Midas Touch*.

HASTING'S VOICE

Blake Barton! That imitation Marlon Brando! Listen, I'm only hiring actors who show up in a suit and without a mouthful of marbles!

27

ELLA

Oh, thanks! I mean—good-bye.

(*Disconnects and starts dialing eagerly, with a delighted chuckle.*)

SUE

Ella! What are you doing?

ELLA

I'm just calling Blake Barton—

SUE

Ella!

BARTON'S VOICE

Hello. Blake Barton here.

ELLA

(*Looks up at* SUE, *shocked and hurt—then speaks in a cold, impersonal voice*)

Susanswerphone.

BARTON'S VOICE

(*With the slurred, faltering diction typical of the legion of would-be Brandos*)

Oh, hiya, girl. Thanks a lot for that tip the other day, but No-Lucksville, Montana. They were lookin' for a Rex Harrison type—English—so I says, "Whatsa matter wi' me? I speak English."

ELLA

(*Frustrated*)

No messages.

BARTON'S VOICE

Crazy, girl.

ELLA

Crazy. (*Disconnects*) You mean I can't even tell him about wearing a suit and about his marbles?

SUE

That's none of your business!

ELLA

Well, if that's what it's going to be like around here, I might as well be back at the Bonjour Tristesse Brassière Company!
(*Pause.*)

SUE

(*Concerned*)

Ella, I'm sorry, but I worry about you. I mean, well all these people on the switchboard you think of as your friends—you don't really know them. They don't care about you—

GWYNNE

And that includes the Sleeping Prince, Ella.

SUE

Yes—Jeffrey Moss—Remember he's just another telephone number, too.

ELLA

(*Sighing, resignedly*)

You're right, all right.
(SUE *works at the table.* GWYNNE *is buried in a magazine.* ELLA *sings, wistfully, to herself*)

29

It's crazy, ridiculous; it doesn't make sense—
But what does he look like?
I wish I knew.
What does he look like?——

(*Music builds to rhythmic climax and blends into sound of a loud phonograph record as the set revolves to* JEFF MOSS' *apartment.*)

SCENE 2

The rather nondescript living room of an expensive East Side bachelor apartment. Stage left are JEFF's *desk and typewriter. Stage right, a few steps lead up to the front door and house phone. Stage center is a large couch. The telephone is on top of a console phonograph to the left of the couch. There is a small but noisy party in progress. About seven couples are dancing, drinking and talking animatedly. One of the guests,* FRANK, *hears the phone ringing above the din and picks it up.*

FRANK
(*Yelling above the racket*)
Hello! Hello! Hey—quiet! (*He switches off the phonograph*) Quiet, everybody! I can't hear. (*Back to phone*) Who? Just a minute. (*He starts walking around the room, looking for the person in question, the long telephone wire trailing behind him*) Jeff! Hey—Jeff! Jeff! Hey—it's for you!
(*A prostrate figure on the couch sits up and takes the phone. It is* JEFF, *who has been hidden by several ladies clustered about him.* JEFF *is an unusually good-looking young man, with a face that reveals both high intelligence and the easy self-indulgence of one who knows he can muddle through life on sheer charm. He dresses carelessly but well. At the moment, he is obviously pleasantly loaded.*)

JEFF

Hello! (*He looks unpleasantly surprised, but continues confidently*) Oh—Olga!—Yeh—Oh—the races! I'm sorry, honey, but I'm having a conference on my play. (*He turns toward his guests and mutters several weird syllables of gibberish reminiscent of crowd noises on a bad radio program. He motions to them to pick it up, and for a few seconds the air is filled with these heated earnest sounds from all—as* JEFF *holds up the phone for good, clear reception. He motions for quiet, much in the manner of a radio director, and resumes his conversation on the phone*) Yeah, I've been working. Call you tomorrow morning, honey. Good-bye.

(*He hangs up.*)

GIRL

Working? Is this the way *all* writers work?

JEFF

Honey, it's not what's on paper that counts. It's what's up here—(*He taps his head significantly*) My play is all ready. One of these days I just crank my ear and it comes out in book form.

ANOTHER GIRL

And wins the Pulitzer Prize, of course—

JEFF

Of course! I have my speech all prepared. (*He puts his arms around two of the girls and speaks in humble but portentous tones*) Gentlemen—today you are honoring me for my maiden solo effort, *The Midas Touch.*—(*Loud applause and cries of "Hear! Hear!"*) But I must decline. (*Murmurs of disappointment*) It is prize enough to know here—(*He indicates the area of his heart*) that I could accomplish this Herculean task without my ex-writing partner, George Livingston, and that I have learned the great lesson of independence.

> (*He leaps upon a chair and, waving a glass of whiskey aloft, sings the following oration*)

You've got to do it!
You've got to do it!
Got to do it all alone.
Just listen to me—
That's the way to be.

Independent, self-sufficient,
Got nobody to rely on.
Independent, self-reliant,
Crave no shoulder I can cry on.
Now I'm livin'—I'm on my own.
Goin' it alone.

I don't need anyone and no one needs me.
No need for anyone to help me
Mix martinis, roast the wienies, bake the blinis
Now that I'm free.

Self-sufficient, self-supporting,
Travelin' light and flyin' solo—
Every day is Independence Day—
Hooray!

Free and easy, blithe and breezy—
Goin' it alone—
I'm independent and on my own.

(The guests cheer him wildly as he downs the toast to himself. At this moment, the house phone rings and JEFF *dashes to answer)*

Hello? What? Larry Hastings?! Tell him I'm not here. Tell him I'm dying. Tell him I went away for the week end. Tell him—

(As he is talking the front door opens and LARRY HASTINGS *enters in time to hear most of the conversation.* LARRY *is a well-dressed, formidable-looking man of about forty.)*

LARRY

Hello, Jeff.

JEFF

(Pleasantly, revealing not the slightest trace of being taken aback)

Hi, Larry! *(Back to phone)* Tell him—never mind, I'll tell him myself. *(With one sweeping gesture, he hangs up, puts his arm around* LARRY *and propels him into room)* Now, Larry, I want to tell you about the second act—

LARRY

(Affably)

I'm sorry to barge in when you're having a party—

JEFF

(Elaborately casual as he mixes LARRY *a drink)*

A party? Couple of friends drop in while I'm taking a five-minute siesta from my work, and he calls it a party! Folks, you all know Larry Hastings— He's my producer! Now, Larry, don't look like ulcers on parade. I've been working. In a couple of days you just back the ol' Mack truck up to the door and we load the script on!

(*He hands* LARRY *the drink.*)

LARRY

(*Grins, and sits heavily on sofa as though planning to stay for several weeks. Then, outdoing* JEFF *in elaborate casualness*)
Well, I'm relieved to hear it. Guess I've been just a finicky old fuss budget—getting so edgy just because I haven't seen a line on paper since that rough first act—six months ago!

JEFF
(*Expansively*)
Why, Lar—I wouldn't let you down. Who's the guy who told me I could write without my partner? And who got Paul Arnold to sign up to star in my play—sight unseen? Larry boy!

LARRY
(*Chuckling*)
Oh, incidentally, Paul Arnold's in town—just got in today—and he can't wait to hear the last two acts, Jeff. I tried to stall him, but I'm afraid you'll have to come to my office—sometime tomorrow—and give him at least an outline. Twelve o'clock all right?

(*Having dropped his bomb, he rises and walks up the steps to the door.*)

JEFF
(*Seemingly unruffled*)
Twelve? (*With a very British accent*) Wizard, old boy! Twelve on the dot!

35

LARRY

(*With a very grim smile*)

And, Jeff—if you don't show, Paul's going to walk. And you
know what else? So am I. I mean it, Jeffie boy. I've had it. It's
your last chance. Well, good night, Jeff.

JEFF

G'night, Larry.

LARRY

(*As he goes*)

Good night, everyone!

JEFF

(*After a somewhat ghastly pause*)

He's a million laughs, once you get to know him. (*Resuming
his party manner*) Well—drink, anyone?
(*The guests—until now frozen—are suddenly galvan-
ized into activity of quick departure. They retreat, hastily
muttering ad-lib good nights.*)

GUEST

(*Leaving*)

I guess we better be going, Jeff—

ANOTHER GUEST

(*Sympathetically*)

Jeff—will you be all right?

JEFF

Sure—sure— A deadline's the best thing for a writer—gives
him *incentive!* Something to aim at! Builds a fire under him—

(*They are gone. He surveys the empty room littered with half-empty glasses and cigarette stubs*) Nothing like a nice cozy fire creeping up your trouser leg! Well—gotta get to work. (*The phone rings*) Oh shut up! (*He answers*) Hullo?

ELLA'S VOICE
(*Mom's voice*)
Mr. Moss, Mr. Hastings called and—

JEFF
Yeah, I know, Mom. He was here. I've got to work tonight—all night. I don't know what time I'll get to sleep, but you've got to wake me at seven o'clock.

ELLA'S VOICE
(*Mom's voice*)
Seven A.M.?

JEFF
Seven A.M.

ELLA'S VOICE
(*Mom's voice*)
Don't worry, Mr. Moss—I'll wake you. Good night!
(*He hangs up. He looks lost—then dials quickly.*)

ELLA'S VOICE
Susanswerphone.

JEFF
Mom?

37

ELLA'S VOICE

(*Changes to Mom's voice, uses it throughout the following telephone conversation*)

Oh, yes—Mr. Moss.

JEFF

Uh—have you got any time to talk to me tonight?

ELLA'S VOICE

Well, I—uh—

JEFF

You know—I thought maybe we could chew the fat for a few minutes— shoot the breeze a bit— I—uh—Mom—I'm afraid.

ELLA'S VOICE

You mustn't be.

JEFF

I know— You've told me that a thousand times—but it's my last chance.

ELLA'S VOICE

Mr. Moss, you can write alone—I know you can—

JEFF

(*With sudden determination*)

Mom, you're right! And I will!

(*He hangs up. With a look of high resolve, he sings to himself in pep-talk fashion, rather grandiosely reminiscent of Nelson Eddy exhorting his stout-hearted men*)

You've got to do it!

You've got to do it!

Got to do it all alone!
No one else'll do it for you—
Buddy Boy! You're on your own.
*(He hurls himself into his chair in front of the typewriter
and is broken out of his manful spell as he takes several
thoughtful swigs of his Scotch and soda)*
Now, let's see— The important thing is to get the first line of
dialogue down on the paper. Harry says—Harry says— *(He
pauses as he picks up his glass again)* I'd better set the scene
first. Griswold's living room—a stuffy Victorian Mansion—
Harry is seated in the armchair, stage right— Lovely touch.
Enter Jenny Brewster. She looks at him; he looks at her. Then
she says—she says— *(He thoughtfully strokes his upper lip
with one finger as he leans forward to typewriter, his face
seemingly set in creative concentration)* Wonder how I'd look
with a mustache—? *(He rises)* Or maybe a beard. No, it would
hurt my tennis game. Boy, I used to hit 'em pretty good. *(He
executes several masterful tennis strokes)* Forehand! Zoom!
Backhand! Whop! Little drinko! *(He drinks)* Whamo! Up
to the net! The winner! *(He leaps imaginary net, and shakes
hands with his imaginary opponent)* Thank you very much.
Actually you play quite well for a loser. Really, you play very—
THE PLAY!
(He rushes back to the typewriter, sings)
You've got to do it!
You've got to do it!
Got to do it all alone!
No one else'll do it for you—
Buddy Boy! You're on your own.
All right—start some place else. Act Three, Scene Two—the
public square. *(Pause. He rises)* Harry mounts the platform.

He looks at the crowd; he clears his throat, and then he says— (*Rushes back to sit at typewriter with fingers poised over keys like a concert pianist*) Harry says—(*He looks down at his fingers*) Wouldn't it be terrible if I froze in this position? (*He rises*) It's the old writer's cramp. That's the trouble with us writers—never get any exercise—maybe a couple of push-ups— (*He stretches out with his feet on the steps and his hands on the floor. He does a brisk push-up and crumples instantly. He pulls himself together painfully and staggers to his feet*) You mustn't overdo it the first day. Oh, well, I can get in shape when the play's on—THE PLAY!

>   (*He rushes back to the typewriter, sings*)
> You've got to do it!
> You've got to do it!
> Got to do it all alone!
> No one else'll do it for you—
> Buddy Boy!

>   (*Suddenly all the Nelson Eddy in him is gone as he gazes
>   dejectedly at the sheets of empty paper before him*)
> Aah, what's the use? I'll never make it alone!

>   (*He disgustedly sweeps the papers off the table. As he
>   slumps in his chair, he reaches for the glass.*)

Curtain

SCENE 3

A disreputable-looking alley at night. Wash hangs on lines; ash cans and general refuse are visible. A nondescript crowd, including some gangster types—a barber, a bootblack, a doorman, a waitress, a pretzel woman, tarts, etc.—are waiting around with a conspiratorial air. SANDOR *enters briskly, carrying his portfolio, and bangs on an ash can with his cane.*

SANDOR

Gentlemen! Gentlemen! (*The crowd comes to attention*) The first meeting of the sales force of Titanic Records Company is hereby called to order. In other words—(*He steps up on box*) Good evening, fellow bookies!

GIRL

What's Titanic Records?

SANDOR

That's us. The new headquarters of our little bookie ring will be located at Susanswerphone—where they are convinced that the Titanic Records Company is a record company. Now, the number one rule is we do not take bets on horses—(*Reaction from crowd*) we take "orders" for records.

GIRL

I don't get it.

SANDOR

(*Passing out charts as he steps down from the box*)
Look these over, gentlemen. Peruse them carefully. Now, Louie, ask me about placing a typical bet—

LOUIE

I'll bet five hundred bucks on the nose on Number 6 in the third race at Belmont.

SANDOR

Splendid! Now consult your charts, gentlemen. As one of the agents for Titanic Records, you would call me up and say, "I would like to place an order (that's bet) for five hundred albums (that's bucks) long playing (that's on the nose) of Beethoven's (that's Belmont) Sixth Symphony (that's horse Number 6) Opus 3 (third race). I would like to place an order for five hundred albums, long playing, of Beethoven's Sixth Symphony, Opus 3!

(*He chuckles and twirls his cane, highly satisfied with himself, and proceeds to teach them his simple little system. The crowd answers his questions, carefully referring to the charts each time.* SANDOR *sings*)

It's a simple little system any child can understand;
The composers' names, we list 'em with the racetracks of the land.
With this simple little system we'll be close by fortune's door—
And to think that no one ever, ever thought of it before!
Gentlemen, look at your charts!

What is Beethoven?

(MAN)

Belmont Park!

(SANDOR)

Where's Puccini?

(MAN)

Pimlico!

(SANDOR)

Who is Humperdinck?

(MAN)

Hollywood!

(SANDOR)

What is Beethoven?

(ALL)

Beethoven is Belmont Park.

(SANDOR)

Where is Puccini?

(ALL)

Puccini is Pimlico.

(SANDOR)

Who is Humperdinck?

43

(ALL)

Humperdinck is Hollyhood.

(SANDOR)

That is correct! Turn the page.

What's Tchaikovsky?

(MAN)

Churchill Downs!

(SANDOR)

Who's Moussorgsky?

(MAN)

Monmouth Park!

(SANDOR)

What's Rachmaninoff?

(MAN)

Rockingham!

(SANDOR)

What's Tchaikovsky?

(ALL)

Tchaikovsky is Churchill Downs.

44

(SANDOR)

Who's Moussorgsky?

(ALL)

Moussorgsky is Monmouth Park.

(SANDOR)

Who's Rachmaninoff?

(ALL)

Rachmaninoff is Rockingham.

(SANDOR)

That is correct! Turn the page

(ALL)

It's a simple little system—we're impatient to begin.
It's a simple little system when the law is list'ning in.

(SANDOR)

We will take those record orders in a very cultured tone,
While we're really booking horses over at Susanswerphone!

(ALL)

We'll be rich! We'll be rich! We'll be rich!
Debussy is Del Mar; Humperdinck is Hollywood.
Cesar Franck is Fair Grounds; Sibelius is Sportsman's Park.
Berlioz is Bainbridge; Hindemith is Hawthorne.
Offenbach is Omaha—

(SANDOR)

Everybody! All together now!

(ALL)

Who is Beethoven?
Belmont Park!
Who's Puccini?
Pimlico!
Who's Tchaikovsky?
Churchill Downs
And Shostakovich is
Sar–a–to–ga!

(SANDOR)

What is Handel?
(*All, suddenly singing to strains from the well-known Handel oratorio*)
Hialeah! Hialeah!

(SANDOR)

Who is Handel?

(ALL)

Hialeah! Hialeah!

Oh, what a system!!!
(*The crowd clusters about* SANDOR, *congratulating him on his ingenious system.*)

Curtain

SCENE 4

Susanswerphone. It is early morning. ELLA *is sleeping in the chair, in pajamas and a robe. The alarm clock on the switchboard sounds. She runs to turn it off.*

ELLA

Seven o'clock! All right, Sleeping Prince.
> (*She takes out a mirror, checks her appearance, then starts dialing* JEFF. *The* TELEPHONE INSTALLATION MAN *enters.*)

TELEPHONE MAN

Titanic Records?

ELLA

Over there. (*He starts to connect the Titanic phones as* ELLA *dials again, a little disturbed because there is no answer*) Why doesn't he answer?
> (THE TELEPHONE MAN *trails wires through the door, and closes it behind him.*)

SUE

(*Cheerily, as she enters with coffee and a bouquet of flowers*)
Good morning!

ELLA

Good morning.

SUE

Brought you some coffee.

ELLA

Thank you.

SUE

Come on. I'll take over. You've been on long enough.

ELLA

(*Uneasily*)

I'm just giving someone his call—

SUE

(*Glancing at call slip, annoyed*)

Jeffrey Moss—*that* one! He takes up more time than all the other subscribers put together! Okay, Ella! All right, Ella! Get up!

(*She pulls out the plug—very impatient with* ELLA— *and practically dumps her out of the swivel chair.*)

ELLA

(*Rising reluctantly*)

Sue, it's a very important wake-up.

(*Ring.*)

SUE

See? Some one was trying to get him. (*She answers as* ELLA, *hovering near, listens*) Jeffrey Moss residence. No, Mr. Hastings. Cannot reach Mr. Moss. What is the message, Mr. Hastings? Yes—(*She writes down message, reading in an impersonal manner as she writes*) Quote.—If you don't show up at noon today with outline, will drop *Midas Touch*. Have taken option on another play. Hope you enjoy trip to Skid Row. Unquote.

ELLA

(*Desperately, trying to get to the switchboard*)
That's a very important message, Sue. He's got to get that message! There must be something wrong!

SUE

(*Forcefully*)
Listen—all this nonsense is over! Just keep remembering one thing— Inspector Barnes. Now, go out! Have a nice day! He's probably unplugged his phone again, anyway.

TELEPHONE MAN

(*Re-entering*)
That's seven dollars and fifty cents for installation.
(SUE *pays him as* ELLA *stands there looking helpless and distressed. Suddenly her face lights up, registering "Eureka!" and she rushes off to change into a street dress.* SANDOR *enters, carrying a bouquet of flowers concealed behind him.*)

SANDOR

Good morning, *Liebchen!*

SUE

Oh, Sandor! (*She rises, hiding her bouquet behind her*) Welcome to Susanswerphone!

SUE *and* SANDOR

(*Extending bouquets simultaneously*)

For you!

(*They laugh uncomfortably and exchange flowers.*)

SANDOR

(*Crossing to his table*)

Splendid board of directors' meeting last night, Sue. (*One of the new phones rings. He sees them*) Ah, my telephones! (*He answers as* SUE *sits at the switchboard*) Titanic Records. Good morning. Yes? Fifteen hundred albums of Puccini's Eighth Piccolo Concerto, Opus 1. Right, we'll ship them right out. (*He hangs up. He picks up the other phone, the direct "warehouse" wire*) Hello. Shipping Department? Fifteen hundred albums of Puccini's Eighth Piccolo Concerto, Opus 1, *all three speeds* (*He hangs up*) See? It's simple. You just pick up the phone, jot down the message, and ring the shipping department on this phone—it's a direct wire—then you give the message just as you get it.

SUE

(*Admiringly*)

Oh, Sandor—do you know all those pieces of music?

SANDOR

(*Modestly*)

I studied under the immortal Tsitsinger.

SUE

(*Giggling girlishly*)

Oh, Sandor, you're a genius!

(*His phone rings again.*)

SANDOR

Your first record order, Sue.
(*He watches as she picks up.*)

SUE

Titanic Records.
(CARL *enters with some coffee from the drug store.*)

CARL

Good morning.
(*He places the order on the table near the door.*)

SUE

(*She writes*)
Thank you. Hello, Carl. (*She picks up the direct wire phone*)
Hello. Shipping Department? Seventy-five albums of Bach's
Third Brandenburg Concerto, Opus 5, LP. Right.

SANDOR

Splendid!

CARL

(*With the avid interest of a record collector*)
Hey—Titanic Records. Is that a new label?

SANDOR

We have only the finest European recordings.

CARL

Oh. Brandenburg Number 3. I have the Fritz Reiner record
ing. Who's on your label?

(*He picks up folder from* SANDOR's *table.* SANDOR *slaps it out of his grasp.*)

SANDOR

(*With enormous authority*)
The Düsseldorf Zyder Zee New Light Hanseatic League Symphony—under Karl Flucht!

CARL

Flucht! Never heard of him.

SANDOR

It's just possible, my dear boy, Flucht never heard of you. Now, please—We are very busy here.

CARL

Sure. Sure. Sorry.
(*He exits.* ELLA *comes out of the bathroom, dressed to go out.*)

SANDOR

'Morning, Ella.

ELLA

(*In a great hurry*)
'Morning.
(*She picks up her shoes near the switchboard and returns to sit in the big chair as* GWYNNE *enters.*)

GWYNNE

Hi. (*To* ELLA) Where you going?
(ELLA *beckons her over for whispered consultation. Ring.* SUE *answers.*)

SUE

Max's Dog and Cat Beauty Shop. Sorry, we don't open till nine o'clock. Thank you.
(*She busies herself, with* SANDOR, *over his books.*)

GWYNNE

(*Horrified whisper*)
Are you out of your mind? Women's Detention Home!

ELLA

Shhhh! Someone has to wake him. I'll just do it and leave.

GWYNNE

The Inspector said no personal contact.

ELLA

It won't be personal. He'll never know who I am.

GWYNNE

How are you going to get in?

ELLA

(*Breathlessly, about to dash out*)
Oh, I'll think of something!
(*Ring.*)

SUE

Ella, take that, please.

ELLA

(*Impatiently plugging in—anxious to leave*)
Women's Detention Home! I mean, Max's Dog and Cat House!

53

THE BELLS ARE RINGING

(She looks horrified as she hears what she has said, drops the phone and dashes for the door.)

Quick Curtain

SCENE 5

The street in front of Susanswerphone. INSPECTOR BARNES *is waiting outside the door.* ELLA, *carrying her handbag, comes running out, unaware of him.*

BARNES

Hello, there! (ELLA *stops dead, as if shot, then starts on*) Hey!
(*He dashes over, blocking her way.*)

ELLA
(*Overly casual*)
Oh, hello, Inspector!

BARNES
(*With an evil, suspicious grin*)
Sorry about our little misunderstanding last night.

ELLA
(*Uneasily, trying to leave*)
That's all right. It could happen to anybody.

BARNES
(*He again blocks her way*)
Where you going?

ELLA

Oh—uh—shopping.

BARNES

Maybe I ought to come along—

ELLA

Oh, that won't be necessary.

BARNES

What are you shopping for?

ELLA

A—a dress—

BARNES

What color?

ELLA

Uh—green!

BARNES

(*Melting*)

Green! Green! My favorite color.

ELLA

(*Relieved, thinking she's free*)

Mine, too.

BARNES

(*Stopping her again*)

I don't know what you're up to, but I'm going to keep my eye on you. You seem to be a pretty confused kid.

THE BELLS ARE RINGING

ELLA

(*Realizing she will have to "con" her way out of his clutches and batting her eyes at him in helpless-ingenue fashion*)

Oh, I am—I'm *very* confused. I need advice. I don't *mean* to be on the wrong side of the law, but sometimes I can't tell right from wrong—I wish you'd help me.

(BARNES *stands puzzled and transfixed as she gradually wears him down with her naïve and helpless questionings—calculated to wrings tears from a stone. She sings*)

Mother and Dad handed down to me
A bit of their old philosophy.
I've stuck to it like an obedient daughter,
But it always lands me in hot water.
I'd gladly follow out your suggestions
If you'd give me the answers
To these questions.
Please tell me—

Is it a crime to start each day
With a laugh and a smile and a song?
And is it a crime to end each day
With a laugh and a smile and a song?
Is it wrong?

Is it a crime to call the world your valentine?
Is it a crime to grab a lamp post
And then sing "Sweet Adeline"—
I ask you—

Is it a crime to save a wee baby bird
When it falls from its nest?

57

That little bird should have a chance
To fly like all the rest.

If it's a crime to help old ladies cross the street,
Then put me in jail!
Without bail!
Bread and water from an old tin pail!
If that—if that's a crime!
Is it a crime—

Inspector Barnes, I'm puzzled
We're taught two things as we go through life:
   One—Be thy brother's keeper
     and
   Two—Mind your own business.

With a laugh and a smile and a song.

Now, if I knew something—and by telling it to someone in
distress,
I could change that someone's life and bring him

The blue bird of happiness—

Is it a crime to tell him?
Or is it a crime not to?
Is it you mustn't
Or—you got to?
Should you say, "Hey, watch out for that banana peel, bud!"?
Or just be silent—then laugh as he

Crashes with a thud—

Inspector Barnes, my job is to get messages to people on
time—

If I have a job
And I see it through,
And it's just my duty
That I do do do,
Is that—is that a—
   (*He wipes away a furtive tear*)
Inspector Barnes—let's go back a few hundred years.
If there had been answering services then—and it had been
   up to me—
I could have prevented many a famous tragedy—
I could have changed the course of history—with a laugh
and a smile and a song.
Why, every night I lie in bed and my cheeks get soaking wet
When I think what I could have done for—
Romeo and Juliet.
   (*She lifts an imaginary telephone*)
Hello. Veronaphone. Oh, yes, Mr. Romeo. Juliet Capulet
called.
The message is: "To avoid marriage with other fellow am
   playing dead. Friar Lawrence gave me great big sleeping
   pill and when I wake up, we'll head for the border." Oh,
   don't thank me. It's all in the day's work—
   (*She hangs up the imaginary phone and turns to* BARNES
   fiercely)
See what I could have done?
Maybe I'm right!
Maybe I'm wrong!
But if I'd got that message through on time,
I'm telling you—

THOSE TWO KIDS WOULD BE ALIVE TODAY!!
So—

> (*With a tremendous sob in her voice*)

If it's a crime to help old ladies cross the street,
Then I'll confess
I'm just a mess—
Mother and Dad, you were wrong—I guess—

> (*In tears*)

Inspector, *were* they wrong?

> (BARNES *is, by now, completely dissolved in tears. He silently pats her shoulder, shaking his head*)

Thank you!

> (*As the music swells, she turns with a dedicated look and starts walking off solemnly—then looks back at the blubbering* BARNES—*and dashes madly off stage as the music builds to a big finish.*)

BARNES

> (*Wiping tears*)

God bless her! There should be more people in the world like her. (*Still tearful, he calls off to* FRANCIS) Francie—

FRANCIS

> (*Entering*)

Yes, Inspector?

BARNES

> (*Suddenly very grim*)

Francie! Follow that girl!!!

Quick Curtain

SCENE 6

JEFF's *apartment.*

JEFF *is still asleep on the sofa, with one hand trailing on the floor. The doorbell is ringing—still, he sleeps. The door opens, and* ELLA *enters cautiously. She approaches* JEFF *and studies his face. As she stands happily stunned by his looks, her purse slides to the floor. Collecting herself, she clears her throat to waken him, but he only turns over. Cautiously, she walks over to the typewriter, takes the sheet of paper out of it, sees it is blank and crumples it in impatience. She takes a bottle off the phonograph, looks at it and bangs it down in disgust. The phonograph suddenly blares forth and she crouches out of sight at the end of the sofa, terrified.* JEFF *leaps up wildly, turns off the machine, and then slumps back on the sofa, clutching his head—a dazed, hung-over, nervous wreck.*

After a moment, ELLA *starts to crawl slowly toward the door, past* JEFF's *sofa, hoping to get by him unnoticed. He sees her out of the corner of his eye and watches tranfixed as she collects her purse and starts to creep up the steps to the door. He sits up slowly and taps her on the shoulder. She turns and they stare at each other.*

ELLA

(Still crouching, very frightened)

Hello.

JEFF

(*Suspiciously*)

Hello.

ELLA

(*Getting up*)

Good-bye.
(*She bolts for the door, but he gets there first and bars the way.*)

JEFF

Hey, wait a minute.

ELLA

I—I must be in the wrong apartment! Well—I—uh—I had this seven o'clock call—I mean an appointment in the wrong apartment. I mean— this isn't 54 Sutton Place South, is it?

JEFF

No. This is 64.

ELLA

(*Trying to assume it's all settled*)

Oh—well—

JEFF

Now, wait a minute. I guess I can either call a cop or go back to sleep.

ELLA

(*Earnestly*)

Oh, don't do that! Please!

JEFF

(Returning to the sofa and curling up)
Never fear—I won't call the police. I give you your freedom.

ELLA

I mean—don't go back to sleep. It's past seven o'clock already.
(She tugs at his ankle.)

JEFF

Look, lady—I don't mind your breaking in here in the
middle of the night—Seven o'clock! I told Mom to call me!
(He springs to the phone.)

ELLA

Excuse me, but your phone is unplugged.

JEFF

Oh—oh, yeah. *(He plugs in cord)* I must have pulled this out
last night when I was looking for something to hang myself
with. *(Ring. He picks up)* Oh, hello, Mom? Oh, you're the
other one. Mr. Hastings called? Taken an option on another
play? He didn't say who's written it— Shakespeare? Tennessee
Williams? Tennessee Ernie? No—never mind. G'bye. *(Hangs
up, depressed. Rises)* Well, I might as well go to sleep forever.
(Notices ELLA *is still there)* G'bye, lady.
(He starts to pour himself a drink.)

ELLA

(A little timidly but determined)
You shouldn't do that.

63

JEFF

What—what did you say???

ELLA

I said, don't do that. You won't be able to do your work.

JEFF

(*Losing his temper rapidly, he takes her arm and ushers her to door*)

Look, lady—I hope you won't be offended if I point out that my evil little habits are not exactly any concern of yours. Now will you please get the hell out of here!

(*He pushes her out.*)

ELLA

You won't do your work!

JEFF

Thank you very much! (*He slams the door and comes back into the room. Stops, thinks and dashes for the door, calling to her*) Miss! (*He opens the door and falls back as* ELLA, *who has been standing just outside, practically falls into the room*) What work?

ELLA

(*Backing him into the room*)

Well, if you want to drink at this hour of the morning, there must be some work you're trying to avoid doing. I know from my own experience. When I had to do my homework in high school, I'd do anything to escape getting down to it. Mostly I'd sharpen pencils—you know, the yellow kind that say Ticonderoga on them? I'd sharpen one down to the Ticonderog—

then Ticonder—then Ticon—and Tico and, finally, Ti and then T—and then I'd have to start on another pencil. Anything but face that awful blank page. (JEFF *glances at his empty type-writer and reaches for a drink.* ELLA *continues, emphatically*) Oh, go ahead and drink! Ruin your *last chance!*

JEFF

(*Taken aback at her use of the phrase*)
Last chance? Last chance to do what?

ELLA

Oh—whatever it's your last chance to do. You look desperate to me.

JEFF

(*Crumbling*)
I'm about to be ill. You don't happen to have a cup of coffee on you do you?

ELLA

(*With a little smile*)
Yes, I do.
(*She takes a large cardboard container of coffee out of her bag, removes the cover, and passes it to* JEFF, *who takes it in open-mouthed astonishment.*)

JEFF

(*Ready for anything*)
And a prune Danish, please.

ELLA

(*Again reaching into her bag, she produces a piece of cheese Danish*)

Cheese.

JEFF

(*By now amused and interested*)

Listen, Miss—uh—

ELLA

(*Improvising swiftly*)

Scott—uh—Melisande.

JEFF

(*Imitating her rhythm*)

Moss—Jefferee. Sit down, Miss Scott.

ELLA

I can't because I have to go.

(*She sits down next to him on the sofa.*)

JEFF

(*Very much interested*)

You know, now that my vision's cleared up and I can make out shapes and colors at six inches, you look pretty good to me. Your appointment doesn't seem very pressing, and I have nothing to do for the next six thousand years or so—

(*He has put his arm around her.*)

ELLA

(*Leaping up*)

That's just another way of avoiding your work—girls!! and you *do* have something to do! You have an appointment!

66

JEFF

Who said so?

ELLA

Your—your seven o-clock call! Now stay up and start writing. You can write alone! You did it once!

JEFF

(*Rising, more and more amazed*)
How do you know I did once?

ELLA

Because—because—anyone who's a writer must have written something by himself once.

JEFF

Did I say I was a writer?

ELLA

No—but—you're not a plumber, are you?

JEFF

No.

ELLA

(*In a tone that implies "it's obvious"*)
Well! But I guess you don't think so yourself or you'd be writing instead of running around all night and coming home at seven in the morning and sleeping all day.

JEFF

(*Staring, astonished*)

It's uncanny. Are you plugged into me somewhere I don't know about?

ELLA

(*Worried*)

No!

JEFF

You know me from some place!

ELLA

No!

JEFF

You're psychic!

ELLA

(*Relieved, she lights up happily*)

Yes! I'm very intuitive. I get feelings about people. I know a lot about you just from listening to you talk—and I get visions and—

(*She stares straight ahead as if in a trance, nodding.*)

JEFF

What's the matter?

ELLA

I've got one now! It's a vision of *you!*

JEFF

What am I doing?

ELLA

(*Tilting her head, still looking at vision*)
Nothing. You're lying face down in the gutter.

JEFF

(*Tilts his head to look too*)
Stop it! You're scaring the hell out of me!

ELLA

I'm sorry. That's what I see and my visions are never wrong—
unless you *do* something—unless you act right now—

JEFF

(*Rising, very disturbed*)
All right. All right! Well, I've tried analysis—why not
witchcraft? All right—I go the witchcraft route! We get the
dolls, the pins, boil the water, get the drums! (*He does a bit
of a drum dance*) You tell me what to do—I do it!

ELLA

(*Rising*)
Keep your appointment!

JEFF

That's no good! I have to turn up with an outline of a whole
play!

ELLA

(*Forcefully*)
You do as I say. Sit down at your typewriter!

JEFF

(Under her spell, he goes to the typewriter)

Yeah?

ELLA

(Standing over him)

And now!!

JEFF

(Eagerly)

Yeah??!!

ELLA

Write it!

JEFF

(Getting up from the typewriter)

I knew there was a catch to it!

(He reaches for his drink.)

ELLA

Oh, stop stalling! You're not so badly off! Why, I know a guy whose father is forcing him to be a dentist when he really wants to be a composer. The poor fellow sits up in his office all day composing songs on the air hose. No one's keeping *you* from doing what you want—except yourself. You're afraid everyone's going to think, "Oh, it was his partner who was the talented one!" So what! You're afraid that what you write won't be important enough, so you don't write anything at all!

JEFF

(Walking away from her, visibly moved by her words)

Boy, do you know me.

70

ELLA

Mr. Moss, you have to have confidence in yourself. I don't even know you, but *I* have confidence in you.

JEFF
(*Looking at her, deeply*)

You do?

ELLA

Yes, I do.

JEFF

You're crazy.

ELLA

Yes, I know.
(*They look at each other for a long moment, then he slowly crosses to the desk and sits down at the type-writer.*)

JEFF

I'll try. (ELLA *picks up her purse and, feeling that her work is done, starts toward the door. He sees that she is going*) I don't think I can do it unless you're here. (*She pauses for a moment, then comes back and sits on the sofa.* JEFF *types*) Act Two, Scene One—Outline—
(*He breathes a heavy sigh, as someone does who has accomplished a tremendous task. The music begins. He starts typing again, stops, pulls the paper out of the machine, crumples it and reaches for a drink. He looks at her, grins sheepishly and returns to work. As he types, she watches him intently, then rises to stand behind him.*)

She starts to place her hands on his shoulders, but withdraws them and just leans over, watching him work, with a radiant, loving smile, as the music builds.)

Curtain

SCENE 7

A street. FRANCIS *is in a phone booth.*

BARNES' VOICE
(*Off stage*)
Inspector Barnes speaking.

FRANCIS
(*Reading excitedly from his report*)
Inspector, she's with a man named Moss—Jeffrey Moss.

BARNES' VOICE
Moss—let's see. He's a subscriber! Number 37. Francis, we're on the right trail!

FRANCIS
Well, they took a cab to a theatrical office building. She waited outside.

BARNES' VOICE
What did she do?

FRANCIS
She bought a bag of peanuts and threw them at some pigeons. Then she had a Fudgicle.

BARNES' VOICE

Is that all?

FRANCIS

No—He came down about an hour later, looking kind of dazed. Then it started to rain—

BARNES' VOICE

Cut the weather report! Where are they now?

FRANCIS

(*Making it all sound ominous and significant*)
Well, he tried to get a cab. She kept saying they'd never get a cab and they should take the subway; he kept saying they'd get a cab, and he ran down the street with her, yelling, "Taxi! Taxi!"

(*The rumble of the subway can be heard, very loud now.*)

The Lights Fade

SCENE 8

The Subway. JEFF *and* ELLA *are standing, center.* JEFF *appears dazed.* ELLA *passes her hand before his face to attract his attention.*

ELLA

What's the matter?

JEFF

He liked it! Larry liked it! I can't believe it!

ELLA

Of course he liked it.

JEFF

Yeah! Well, he isn't exactly tearing out the front page. He had a couple of criticisms—and he pointed out that it isn't exactly written yet. He made me promise I'd go to the country for a week and work. But by and large, it's something of a miracle.

ELLA

It is not a miracle. You did it.

JEFF

You know what?

75

ELLA

What?

JEFF

(*Turning her toward him and looking into her eyes*)
You're the miracle! (*The subway lurches to a stop, doors open, people pour in, pushing and jostling.* ELLA *and* JEFF *are separated in crowd. They push toward each other until they are again together.* JEFF *looks around with displeasure*) Look—people.

ELLA

What did you expect? Herrings?
(*Another jolt. A man comes between them.*)

JEFF

But I feel like celebrating the miracle! (*Turns to her and finds himself face to face with the man. Pushes him aside.* ELLA *and* JEFF *exchange looks*) Do you mind? We ought to be some place—alone—or at least with some congenial people!
(*A man—a real horror with a sour face—turns to face front.*)

ELLA

We have a car full of them.

JEFF

Congenial! This band of cut-throats? Did you ever see such hatred? If I asked any one of them for the time of day, this would turn into a lynch mob.

76

ELLA

(*Laughing*)

Everybody wants to be friendly but nobody wants to make the first move. Why don't you say hello to that nice man over there? He'd appreciate it.

(*She points to "the horror."*)

JEFF

Him? That's Dracula's uncle—the Wolf Man. The only thing he'd appreciate would be a nice fresh cup of blood.

ELLA

It would be so easy. All you'd have to do would be to say hello. Watch. (JEFF *shakes his head incredulously at her. She crosses in front of* JEFF) Hello.

(*"The horror" turns with a look as though he'd eat her.*)

MAN

What did you say?

ELLA

I only said hello.

MAN

(*Amazed, and then starting to sob*)

Hello? Hello? Did you say hello? This—this—is the first time anyone said hello to me on the subway in thirty years! Hello! (*Shakes her hand, grinning*) My name is Ludwig Smiley.

ELLA

How do you do, Mr. Smiley. I'd like you to meet Mr. Moss.

77

SMILEY (MAN)

Hello!

JEFF
(*Incredulously*)

Hello.

SMILEY

(*To another man*)
Hello. My name is Ludwig Smiley!

OTHER MAN
(*Beaming*)

Hello. I'm Charles Bessemer.

(CHARLES BESSEMER, *in turn, says hello to the person next to him, and soon everyone is shaking hands with everyone else, happily shouting hello's. Each new person who has his hand shaken reacts suspiciously for a fleeting moment, then, happily delighted at this unexpected outburst of friendship, shakes hands and "hello's" whoever is nearest him. The happy buzz of conversation spreads like wildfire as people start moving about, waving across the car, and making new friends.*

JEFF *looks about him, amazed and pleased, as he and* ELLA *join in the general handshaking and greetings. The occasion suddenly assumes all the aspects of a party as everyone sings a gang song of camaraderie.*)

(ALL *sing, still shaking hands with one another*)
Hello, hello there!
Pleased to meet you!
It's a pleasure and a privilege!

Glad to know you!
How are you? Hello!

Hello, hello there!
Pleased to meet you!
It's a pleasure and a privilege!
Glad to know you!
How are you? Hello!
    (FIRST MAN)
Let's have a party
And pour out the wine!
    (SECOND MAN)
I've got salami!
    (THIRD MAN)
So everything's fine!
    (ALL)
Let's sing together
And let out a yell
'S always fair weather
When we're singing—

Hello, hello there!
Pleased to meet you!
It's a pleasure and a privilege!
Glad to know you!
How are you? Hello!
    (*As the party progresses, there are sudden lurches when
the train stops and a new batch of strap-hangers enter.
They, too, are greeted with hello's and handshakes and
quickly join in the fun. The carnival spirit grows—and
finally, a group of four men enter and, as they become*

a part of the party, rapidly rip off their outer clothing, revealing the flamingly colorful costumes of acrobats. They are teeter-board artists. As one of the acrobats prepares to be hurtled off the end of the teeter board and land on a chair that is being held aloft by two of his fellow performers, the train lurches, there is a sudden blackout, and, as the lights go on again, we see that in some mysterious manner, instead of the acrobat, ELLA has been catapulted above into the chair. She graciously acknowledges the cheers of the crowd and the curtain closes on a final rousing chorus of the song.)

Quick Curtain

Scene 9

A street. The sun is shining brightly. Many of the people from the subway, including JEFF *and* ELLA, *are emerging into the street. They are still bubbling with high spirits.*

JEFF
(*Laughing*)
That's the best party I've been to in years. Hostess, thank you.

ELLA
You're welcome. Drop in any time.

JEFF
(*Looking up as if seeing some new cosmic phenomenon*)
Hey! The sun! This is the first time I've seen the sun in years. Mom would never believe this! Hey, let's call her!

ELLA
(*Transfixed*)
Who?

JEFF
Mom! That's the little old lady at my answering service.

ELLA

(*Brought back to reality and covering up*)
Oh. Oh! I—I—Where are we? Fifty-third Street? I have to
go out to Bay Ridge!

JEFF

Bay Ridge?

ELLA

Yes. I spend a lot of time out there—taking care of my uncle.

JEFF

Uncle!

ELLA

You don't believe I have an Uncle Gus in Bay Ridge?

JEFF

Sure. If you told me the world was flat, I'd believe you. You're
the only honest person I ever met in my life.

ELLA

(*Troubled*)
Honest person.

JEFF

(*Looking at her tenderly, deeply*)
If I couldn't believe in you—after all this—I'd crumble away
like a piece of stale sponge cake.

ELLA

(*Very disturbed*)
Then believe me—I have to go.

JEFF

But I'll be gone for a week. When'll I see you?

ELLA

I don't know.

JEFF

I'll call you from the country.

ELLA

No phone.

JEFF

Now wait a minute! You promise I see you a week from today—or I don't go at all. In fact, I tail you to Bay Ridge right now!

(*Agreeing ad libs from the interested onlookers.*)

ELLA

All right. All right! Your place—next Wednesday—six o'clock.

JEFF

Promise?

ELLA

Promise. (*He kisses her cheek. She looks back at him, moved*) Good-bye.

JEFF

Good-bye. (*She exits.* JEFF *calls after her*) Wednesday—six o'clock. And don't forget to bring the cheese Danish!

83

(He turns to center stage and, full of exuberance, sings out)

YAHOO!
I met a girl—
A wonderful girl!
She's really got a lot to recommend her for a girl,
A fabulous creature without any doubt.
Hey! What am I getting so excited about?!

She's just a girl—
An ev'ry day girl.
And yet I guess she's really rather special for a girl,
For once you have seen her the others are out.
Hey! What am I getting so excited about?!

But so what? What has she got others have not?
Two eyes, two lips, a nose—
Most girls have some of those.
Yet when she looks up at me, what do I see?
The most enchanting face! My pulse begins to race. Hey!

I met a girl—
A marvelous girl!
She's rarer than uranium and fairer than a pearl.
I found me a treasure and I want to shout!
This is what I'm getting so excited about!
I met a girl and I fell in love today!

(He is carried off aloft by the cheering crowd.)

Curtain

SCENE 10

DR. KITCHELL'S *office.* DR. KITCHELL *is a sweet, ineffectual-looking, balding young man with glasses. He is playing a tune on the air hose. Then he sings as he writes it down.*

(KITCHELL)
I love your sunny teeth—
Your funny, sunny teeth—
They're like a pearly wreath
That hangs over my heart!

ELLA
(*Entering*)
Hello.

KITCHELL
(*Surprised at the strange face*)
Hello?

ELLA
(*Staring at him, delighted to meet him*)
So you're Dr. Kitchell, the dentist!

KITCHELL
(*Puzzled*)
Yeah, isn't it wonderful! I'm sorry, I forgot we had an appointment. Won't you sit down? What did you say your name is?

ELLA

(Sitting in chair)
It started hurting as I was coming down the hall.

KITCHELL

Oh, all rightee—*(Strikes dental mirror on tray, listens as if to a tuning fork and hums an "A")* Open wide, please. *(Looks in her mouth with the mirror)* I don't see anything.

ELLA

But it hurts.
 (KITCHELL, suddenly transfixed, sings, soupy-ballad style, staring ecstatically into space)
You don't see anything, but it hurts.
Though you can't see the pain in my heart—
Oh—oh—how it hu–u–rts!
 (Returning to reality, he again addresses ELLA*)*
Is it sensitive to hot and cold?

ELLA

Ummm—hmmm.
 (KITCHELL, again inspired, sings a rythmic tune)
First you're hot—then you're cold,
Then you're shy—then you're bold,
But I'm always sensitive to you–ooooo!

ELLA

Gee, those songs are pretty.

86

KITCHELL

(*Excited*)

Did you like them?

ELLA

Oh, yes!

KITCHELL

You're the first one. I lose more patients this way. I'm a terrible dentist. I make up songs all the time—and I can make up songs about anything—anything at all. Just give me a subject—a title—anything. What are you thinking of right now? Right off the top of your head!

ELLA

(JEFF *on her mind*)

Sponge cake!

KITCHELL

Sponge cake?

ELLA

No—uh—*The Midas Touch!*

KITCHELL

Ah. "The Midas Touch"—about a king—and the gold—and —that's simple.

(*He starts singing*)

The Mi—das Touch!

The mighty—mighty—mighty Midas Touch!

That Midas wanted gold so much—

ELLA

(*Interrupting*)

That's brilliant! Well, I guess you'll be there.

KITCHELL

Huh? Where?

ELLA

Pyramid Club. Friday at ten o'clock. They're auditioning songs.

KITCHELL

(*Bursting with excitement*)

I'll be there at nine-thirty.

(FRANCIS *has appeared at the transom over the door. He snaps a picture.*)

ELLA

You write that down now.

(*As* KITCHELL *writes, she slips out the door.*)

KITCHELL

(*Turning around*)

Golly, I don't know how to thank—(*She has disappeared. He goes to the door, opens it, calling*) Oh, miss! Oh, miss! (*Then, suddenly inspired again, he sings*)

Oh, Mississippi steamboat rounding the bend—

Whooo! Whooo!

(*He rushes to write it down.*)

Quick Curtain

Scene 11

A street. BARNES *and* FRANCIS *enter.* BARNES *is looking at a picture and checking the subscriber list.*

BARNES

Let's see—uh-huh—Dr. Kitchell— Number 33—

FRANCIS

Inspector, I'm sure she ain't no lady of the evening.

BARNES

(*Thinking*)

Kitchell. A dentist, huh? I've got it! It's a front for baby-selling racket. Come on.

FRANCIS

She seems like such a nice girl—
(*They start off, but turn aside as* KITCHELL *enters, carrying sheet music—on his way to the audition—and crosses hurriedly, looking for an address.* FRANCIS *follows him.* BARNES *exits in the opposite direction.*)

Quick Curtain

A drug store. Several "Brando's," all dressed alike in jeans and leather jackets, are lounging about, reading Show Business, Variety, *etc. Two of them exchange inarticulate grunts, "Uhhh," while looking at* Variety. *The* CLERK *is behind the counter.* BLAKE BARTON *enters, dressed like the others. When he speaks, it is with the hesitant, slurred speech these actors* think *is an imitation of their idol.*

GUYS

Uhnhh—

BARTON

Uhnhh—

ONE GUY

Hey, Barton, did ya get da part in *The Midas Touch?*

BARTON
(*Strokes his hair down on his forehead*)
Naah. How about you guys?

GUYS
(*Stroking their hair with the same gesture*)
Sssss. Naah!

90

BARTON

(*Going toward the counter. In the "Hey, Stella" delivery*)
Hey, Jooeeey—

CLERK

(*Wearily*)

Yes, sir!

BARTON

Gimme—uh—uh chocolit sundae—with the hot fudge
action—and look, honey boy—(*Grasps him by lapels*) no
crushed nuts. One crushed nut and, man, I'm steamed—
  (ELLA, *wearing flats and leather jacket and motorcycle
  cap, enters. All look at her; all scratch their stomachs;
  *ELLA *scratches with them, in rhythm.*)

ELLA

(*Speaking like the rest of them*)
Whose motorcycle 'sat out there?

ONE GUY

'At's Barton's.

BARTON

Crazy, ain't it?

ELLA

(*Snaps fingers and kicks*)
Cuckoo—

ALL

(*Same gesture*)
Cuckoo.

ELLA

(*To the* CLERK)

Hey, Fellaaaa! Gimme unhh double banana split—two scoops
with plenny the jazz—anna extra saucer for my marbles.
(*Takes several marbles from her mouth and deposits them in
saucer which the* CLERK *holds out to her*) So you're Barton,
huh? Havin' any luck?

BARTON

(*He takes from his pocket a white woolen mitten and pulls it
on while speaking*)

Naah—Thought I had a chance at that new show, *The Midas
Touch.* I coulda been a contender—but—I—I—dunno—

GUYS

(*Doing the same with mittens*)

Uhhh—I dunno—

ELLA

D' j' ever try wearing a suit?
(*All freeze, shocked.*)

BARTON

What? I can't do that! What d'ya take me for? A traitor?
We gotta name for actors dat wear suits. I ain't turnin' Walter
Pidgeon for nobody.

ELLA

Sure! Be a punk imitation the rest of your life! I'm tellin'
ya! If you want da job, you gotta cut da blue jeans action!
Look around ya! You're a glut on the market. You're *nothin'!*
(BARTON *looks around at the others, realizing the truth*

in this. At this point, FRANCIS *appears, snaps a picture and exits, unnoticed.*)

BARTON

Okay! You're right! I'll do it!

ELLA

(*Happily, resuming her own speaking voice*)
Brooks Brothers! Forty-fourth and Sponge Cake!—*Madison!*

BARTON

Cuckoo!

ELLA

Cuckoo!
(*She exits.*)

BARTON

All right, come on, fellas! On to Brooks Brothers! (*They turn from him as from a leper*) Okay! I'm not afraid of you. I'm going all the way! (*In a strong British accent*) Tennis anyone? (*He does a royal ballet leap and flies out the door.*)

Curtain

SCENE 13

A street. BARNES *and* FRANCIS *enter.* BARNES *is checking the subscriber list.*

BARNES

Number 52. Blake Barton. We got an actor, a dentist—I got it! She's probably pushin' dope! It's a dope ring!

FRANCIS

But she seems like such a nice girl.

(*They start off, but turn aside as* BARTON *enters and crosses hurriedly with a Brooks Brothers box under his arm.* FRANCIS *follows him off.* BARNES *exits in the opposite direction.*)

Curtain

SCENE 14

Susanswerphone. It is one week later. SANDOR *is talking on the* *Titanic phone;* GWYNNE *is at the switchboard;* SUE *is seated at* *the table near the center door.*

GWYNNE

No, this is not Telanswerphone. This is Susanswerphone.

SANDOR

Yes. Yes, that's fifteen hundred copies of Beethoven's Tenth Symphony, Opus 6, all speeds. Yes. Yes, that makes five thousand three hundred orders in all today on Beethoven's Tenth. Yes, we've had a splendid week.

(*He hangs up and goes toward the door.*)

SUE

(*Stopping him*)

Sandor—

SANDOR

I was just on my way to watch them run off the Beethoven pressings at the Long Island plant. See you at dinner, *Liebchen. Aufwiedersehen!*

SUE

Bye, bye! (SANDOR *steps aside to let* ELLA *enter, then goes out.* ELLA *looks worried*) Hi, Ella.

ELLA

(*Subdued*)

Hi. I'll take over, Gwynne.

GWYNNE

(*Rises.* ELLA *sits at the switchboard.* GWYNNE *sits in the big chair*)

What's the matter, Ella?

ELLA

Oh—nothing.

SUE

Well, see you later, girls. I'm off to the bank. *Aufwiedersehen!*

(*She exits. Ring.*)

ELLA

(*Plugging in*)

Mr. Linden's residence.

VOICE

Hello. This is Miss Penny. Did he leave a message? For me?

ELLA

Yes, Miss Penny. Mr. Linden will pick you up at twelve-thirty. He said to wear something high-priced and low-cut. It's a small party at the Gilbert Millers' for Ali Khan, Betty Kean and Harry Cohn.

VOICE

Thank you. Good night.

ELLA

Good night. (ELLA *unplugs. The Titanic phone rings; she picks it up as* CARL *enters with an order and places it on the table*) Titanic Records.

GWYNNE

Hi, Carl.

CARL

Hi.

ELLA

Yes? (*Writing*) Three hundred copies of Beethoven's Tenth Symphony, Opus 6, LP. Thank you.

GWYNNE

Boy, is that a popular piece.

CARL

Hey, there must be a mistake in that order. Beethoven only wrote nine symphonies.

ELLA

Really?

GWYNNE

But there've been so many orders for Beethoven's Tenth today.

CARL

They gotta mean the Ninth. Tchaikovsky—six, Brahms—four, and Beethoven—nine.

97

ELLA

Well, you sure know your music. I better tell the shipping department, huh? (*She dials.* GWYNNE *pays* CARL) Hello, shipping? I have an order for three hundred albums of Beethoven's *Ninth* Symphony, Opus 6, LP. Yes—and, look—change all the other orders you have for Beethoven's Tenth to Beethoven's *Ninth*. Sure I'm sure—(*Looks at* CARL, *who makes a reassuring gesture*) absolutely sure. Thank you. (*She hangs up*) Thanks, Carl.

CARL

Any time.
(*He exits.*)

GWYNNE

Well, now, who's on the outpatient list for today?

ELLA

Nobody!

GWYNNE

I know what's bothering you. This is Wednesday, six o'clock —one week later—the return of George Bernard Moss.

ELLA

(*Trying to cover her feelings*)
Nothing is bothering me. I'm never going to see him again.

GWYNNE

But you made a date with him for tonight.

ELLA

But I'm not going to keep it. He thinks I'm the most honest person who ever lived. He never believed in anybody before. I *can't* tell him the truth. I can't! I'm not going to crumble the sponge cake!

GWYNNE

The what?

ELLA

(*Trying to assume a light air*)
I got a good look at him—got him to work— Mission accomplished. I'm going to forget about him. Never going to see him again—couldn't care less. (*Ring.* ELLA *answers*) Susanswerphone.

JEFF'S VOICE

Hello. Mom?
(*At the sound of his voice,* ELLA *crumbles inside. She holds out the headpiece to* GWYNNE, *then snatches it back.* GWYNNE *leans on the switchboard.*)

ELLA

(*Controlling herself. In Mom's voice*)
Yes, Mr. Moss?

JEFF'S VOICE

(*Bright and exhuberant*)
Listen, Mom—I've only got a minute—I'm unpacking, but I wanted to call you to thank you for the insane faith you've had in me. I have a chance of coming through for you, after all. Got nearly two acts done. Don't know if they're any good, but they're there.

ELLA

That's good, Mr. Moss.

JEFF'S VOICE

Say, Mom—have there been any messages from a Melisande Scott?

ELLA

(*Controlled*)

No, Mr. Moss. Absolutely none.

JEFF'S VOICE

Oh, well, I have a date with her for this evening.

OLGA'S VOICE

Hello, Jeffrey!

(ELLA *freezes and gasps.*)

JEFF'S VOICE

Olga—how did you get in here?

OLGA'S VOICE

Oh, darling, I've been waiting for you. Oh, sweetheart— Oh, Jeffrey!

JEFF'S VOICE

(*Hurriedly*)

Well—I—uh—call you back, Mom!

(*He hangs up.* ELLA *unplugs, jumps up, snatches her purse and dashes for the door. Suddenly she stops and almost sits on a chair. She starts and stops several times— hesitating, frantic.*)

GWYNNE

What's the matter?

ELLA

(*Very offhand*)

Nothing.

(*Suddenly* ELLA *lets out a hoarse animal scream, reminiscent of Sir Laurence Olivier's famous anguished cry in* Oedipus Rex, *and dashes out.*)

(*As the music comes up strong, the set revolves to* JEFF'S *apartment.*)

SCENE 15

JEFF's *apartment. Olga, a flashy brunette, is with* JEFF. *He carries bags to a closet and puts them inside. He looks healthy, businesslike and well organized.*

OLGA

Oh, don't be a pill, Jeffrey. You can work some other time. They're waiting for us downstairs.

JEFF

(*Impatiently*)

Look, Olga. I'm not taking you to the trotting races in Yonkers. I have a business appointment here.

OLGA

Business appointment—Ha!

JEFF

And I've got to work!

OLGA

Look—if you think you're going to get rid of me that easily—

(ELLA *enters, slamming the door.*)

JEFF

(*Happy*)

Mel!

ELLA

(*Breathless*)

Hello, Mr. Moss!

OLGA

Business appointment! Ha!

ELLA

(*A demon*)

I'm Mr. Moss's secretary. (*Crosses to* OLGA, *backs her toward the door, imitating* OLGA's *screechy voice*) Listen, Mr. Moss has work to do. You're not going to waste his time dragging him to the *races*. Get somebody else to take you to the *races*. (OLGA *flops back on the steps, dumbfounded*) Now, where *were* we, Mr. Moss? (*Goes to typewriter and sits down, very business-like*) Act Twelve, Scene Nine, wasn't it?

JEFF

(*Going along with it*)

Yes, Act Twelve, Scene Nine— (OLGA, *stunned, stares open-mouthed.* JEFF *helps her up*) You see, I really do have to work, Olga. Good-bye. Call you some time. (*He see her out. He looks at* ELLA) Hey, how'd you know about her—and the races?

ELLA

(*Contemptuously*)

It was written all over her face. She even looks a little like a horse.

JEFF

I can't believe it. You're really here.

ELLA

(*Gets up from typewriter uneasily, suddenly conscious of where she is*)

I can't believe it, either.

JEFF

(*Also a little uneasy*)

Well, now that she's out of the way—let's take it from the top, where you come in the door and I say, "How are you, Mel?"

ELLA

I'm fine, thank you. How are you?

(*They are standing, somewhat uncomfortably, in the middle of the room.*)

JEFF

I'm fine, thank you.

(*They shake hands.*)

ELLA

(*Formally*)

How did your work go?

JEFF

Well, I didn't quite do five million pages. I rewrote the first act—and finished more than half the second—and only threw up forty or fifty times a day. It went quite well, actually. (*She looks troubled*) What's the matter?

ELLA

Nothing.
(*He starts toward her.*)

JEFF

Oh—Mel—

ELLA

(*Avoiding him*)
Oh, no!

JEFF

What is this! What did you come back for, anyway?!

ELLA

I thought you needed a secretary.

JEFF

A secretary!

ELLA

You're pretty well fixed for girls. But I guess you don't really need me so—so—I'll—
(*She tries to get her purse from the sofa. He blocks her path.*)

JEFF

(*Brusquely*)
All right—if you're here as a secretary—then get to the type-writer! What do you charge?

ELLA

Nothing!

JEFF

Come on!

ELLA

(*Angry and tense*)
Oh—a thousand dollar an hour!

JEFF

(*Looking at her, saying the first thing that comes to him*)
That sounds reasonable enough—and don't worry—I'll keep my grimy paws off you. Sit down! (*She sits, tentatively. He paces restlessly*) Where were we? Act Twelve, Scene Nine. Senor Mendoza's Hacienda in Iceland. Old faithful Rodriguez is kneeling by his bedside. Never mind that—(*Stops and begins again tenderly*) Would you take down this message, please? It's to a girl—"Dearest"—that's the beginning of the message—
　　(*He sings*)
Dearest—Dearest—
One thing I know—
Everything I feel for you
Started many years ago.

Long before I knew you—
Long before I met you—
I was sure I'd find you
Some day, some how.
I pictured someone who'd walk and talk and smile as you do,
Who'd make me feel as you do right now!

But that was long before I held you,
　　(*He crosses to stand behind her*)
Long before I kissed you,

Long before I touched you and felt this glow;
    (*Places hands on her shoulders*)
But now you really are here and now at last I know
That long before I knew you,
I loved you so.

ELLA

Is that all?

JEFF

But you didn't write anything down.

ELLA

I didn't have to—
    (*She sings*)
Long before I knew you—
Long before I met you—
I was sure I'd find you
Some day, some how.
I pictured someone who'd walk and talk and smile as you do,
Who'd make me feel as you do right now!
    (*He touches her cheek. She gets up, agitatedly, picks up*
    her purse and starts for the door. She speaks)
I really have to go!

JEFF

Mel, you can't! You dropped into my life like a miracle! You
saved me when I was drowning! You can't throw me back to
the sharks! (*Simply*) Mel—I love you.
    (*She hesitates, then dashes out. He sinks to the sofa,*
    dejected. Suddenly, the door opens and ELLA *returns.*)

ELLA

(*Looking like the Statue of Liberty holding the beacon aloft*)
If it's a crime to help old ladies cross the street—
  (*She throws down her purse and leaps into* JEFF's *arms
  They kiss passionately and happily as* FRANCIS *slips in
  the door, snaps picture and exits.*)

Curtain

Act Two

Act Two

Scene 1

Susanswerphone. The following night. ELLA *is seated at the switchboard in a resplendent ball gown. It contrasts ludicrously with the drabness of her surroundings, as does her regal bearing and proud, queenly smile. The gown looks a little too theatrical for any normal surroundings. It clearly suggests grand oprea and is, in fact,* MADAME GRIMALDI's *ball gown from* La Traviata. GWYNNE, *seated at stage left, is eyeing it dubiously as the phone rings.*

ELLA
(Picks up and speaks in a haughty British accent)
The Duchess of Windsor's residence.

VOICE
Is the Duchess in?

ELLA
The Duchess won't be back till after Labor Day.

VOICE
Thank you.

111

ELLA

Not at all!

(*She unplugs the phone, rises and twirls about the stage, humming an air from* Traviata *as* SUE *enters.*)

SUE

Oh, Ella! You look absolutely radiant! Like something out of *Traviata!* (ELLA *is deflated for an instant*) Something's happened to you since yesterday. You got in real late last night, didn't you?

ELLA

I'm sorry—

SUE

Oh, I'm tickled! If you found a fella you like—well, that's wonderful! (*Giggling*) I should know! (*To* GWYNNE) Well— I'll be back a little later to relieve you, Gwynne. (*To* ELLA) Have a good time, honey!

(*Kisses a finger and places it on* ELLA's *cheek.*)

ELLA

You, too.

(*She returns the kiss.* SUE *exits.*)

GWYNNE

Yesterday it was "man overboard." What's your excuse for seeing him tonight?

ELLA

Woman overboard! And—besides—I can't let Madame Grimaldi's gown go to waste.

GWYNNE

And he still doesn't know you're the dear little old lady of the switchboard?

ELLA

(*Suddenly troubled*)

No. I—I meant to tell him last night. But somehow I forgot. But I'll tell him tonight. I'll find the right moment and I'll just tell him. It shouldn't be so hard to do, should it, Gwynne? Should it?

GWYNNE

(*Dubiously*)

Good luck, honey. (*Steps on* ELLA's *dress and it rips when* ELLA *moves*) Dandy. Here we better shorten that.

(*She helps* ELLA *up on the chair and rips off the lower ruffle.* CARL *enters with two sinister-looking men. They are the* HENCHMEN *of the Corvello mob, the racing syndicate for which* SANDOR *works.*)

CARL

(*To the* HENCHMEN)

Is this the place you mean?

HENCHMAN

Is Sandor around?

ELLA

He's at the Crying Gypsy Cafe.

HENCHMAN

Let's go.
(*The men exit.*)

CARL
(*Looking at* ELLA)

Wow!

ELLA

Thanks.

CARL
(*Yelling up to the street*)
Hey, Pedro! Get a load of Ella!
(*Down come several neighborhood characters who look at* ELLA. *They ad-lib, indicating excitement and approval.*)

BOY

Hey! Where ya goin'? That's some dress!

GIRL

Oh, Ella! You look beautiful! Goin' to some big fancy society ball?

ELLA
(*Charmingly offhand*)
No. Just a friend and myself. Just two of us—El Morocco, Pyramid Club—who knows?

CAROL
(*One of the neighborhood girls, enters, carrying an evening purse*)
Hey, Ella—here it is! Does it go with it all right?

114

ELLA

(*Taking the purse, delighted*)

Perfect! Thanks, Carol.

ANOTHER BOY

(*Entering with a red handkerchief*)

Here's the handkerchief. My ma just finished ironing it.

GWYNNE

And don't lose this. It's copied from a very good copy.

(*She puts a bracelet on* ELLA's *wrist.*)

CARL

(*Chagrined*)

And *I* got *nothing* to give you. Hey! Maybe you could use a cha-cha lesson. You can't go dancing unless you know the cha-cha!

ELLA

(*Defiantly*)

I can mambo!

CAROL

Not the same thing!

CARL

You're dead if you can't cha-cha! Free lesson! Look!

(CARL *and* CAROL *beat out the rhythm with their hands;* ELLA *picks it up.*)

ELLA

What about my feet? (*They teach her the basic steps. At one*

point they do a more intricate step. She stops) Sneaks! (*They all resume the simpler routine*) I've got it! I've got it!
(*They lead her to a chair.*)

BOY

Now you're at the Pyramid Club.

ELLA

I'm at the Pyramid Club.

GIRL

And Carl's going to be there and he'll ask you to dance.

ELLA

Oh, you're going to be there, Carl?

GIRL

No—It's a game.

ELLA

Oh, it's a game and I'm at the Pyramid Club and Carl's going to ask me to dance. Okay.

(CARL *has removed his jacket, revealing a gaily colored shirt, and has picked up a straw hat. He seems suddenly transformed into a slinky, Latin-type male.*)

(CARL SINGS)

Aye, yi, yi, yi, yi!

(ELLA)

Aye, yi, yi, yi, yi!

(CARL, *insinuatingly*)

Mu-cha-cha, tell me, do you cha-cha?

(ELLA, *in a coy, high squeak*)

Me-cha-cha? Señor, si-si cha-cha.

(CARL)

Now, cha-cha, please show me how cha-cha.

(ELLA)

I got-cha—You watch-a cha-cha.
(*She rises and they dance during the following.*)

(CARL)

Hey, cha-cha, is this the way cha-cha?

(ELLA)

Si! Oh, cha-cha, away we go cha-cha.

(CARL)

Ay, cha-cha; I'm feeling high cha-cha.

(BOTH)

Oh, such a
Hot-cha-cha
Cha-cha

(ELLA)

Come a little closer, then a little closer,
Then you turn and walk away.
Ay yi!

(BOTH)

Ta ta tum ta ta ta ta ta ti-ga ti-ga
Tum ta ta ta ta ta tiga-tiga
Tum ta ta ta ta ti-ga tiga
Tum ta ta ta ta ta ti-ga ti-ga

(CARL)

Come a little closer, then a little closer.
Don't go way, my little mu-cha-cha—
The dance is through, cha-cha.

(ELLA)

Now, cha-cha, let's have some chow, cha-cha.

(CARL)

Then, cha-cha, we'll dance again, cha-cha.

(BOTH)

Closer and closer
And closer and closer
And closer and closer to you,
Mu-cha-cha!

(ELLA *exits, cha-cha-ing madly, to the cheers of her friends, who, caught up in the spirit of the rhythm they have created, continue their dancing, temporarily turning Susanswerphone into a Cuban dance hall.*)

Curtain

SCENE 2

A street bordering the park. At night. In the background are trees and a vista of the New York skyline. JEFF, *in evening attire, is seated on a bench, waiting for* ELLA. *A man crosses.* JEFF, *with sudden happy inspiration, sings, "Hello, hello there!" as the man passes. The latter turns and looks at him with disbelief and extreme suspicion, then dashes off.* JEFF *shrugs and laughs, amused. At this point* ELLA *comes on—an unusual sight in her red ball gown, especially since she is still determinedly executing the cha-cha and muttering the steps to herself.* JEFF *rises, a trifle taken aback.*

ELLA
(Breathlessly)
Hello. One—two—cha-cha-cha.

JEFF
Hello. *(She continues to dance)* Hey, wait a second!

ELLA
I've just learned this. I don't want to lose it.

JEFF
(Laughing)
Don't you want to hear the news? Larry liked all the stuff!

119

ELLA

(*In cha-cha rhythm*)

Good! Good! Good, good, good!

(*She sits, but continues the steps with her feet.*)

JEFF

And Paul Arnold, our star, is here from Hollywood.

ELLA

Oh, good!

JEFF

And Larry's giving a big party for Paul tonight.

ELLA

Good! I hope they all have a swell time.

JEFF

And we have to go—

ELLA

(*Stopping suddenly*)

Oh, no!

JEFF

I have to, darling. Paul Arnold's the star of my play.

ELLA

(*Uneasy*)

But—but I don't know any of those famous people—

JEFF

So you'll meet them.

ELLA

I don't want to.
(*She rises and starts dancing again.*)

JEFF

Hey, I met all *your* friends on the subway. Don't be such a snob!
(*She stops, laughs.*)

ELLA

(*Referring to her dress*)
But—is *this* all right?

JEFF

It's magnificent—like something out of *Traviata*. (*Seeing her look suddenly crestfallen, he kisses her*) You look lovely.

ELLA

But I thought we were going to go dancing—just the two of us.

JEFF

All right, let's dance.

ELLA

Where?

JEFF

Right here.

ELLA

In the park?

JEFF

What's the matter? No guts?
(*He starts dancing her madly across the stage.*)

ELLA

(*Laughingly protesting*)
Stop it!

JEFF

Don't you like dancing?

ELLA

I love it!
(*She snuggles close and they dance a few steps quietly.*)

JEFF

Actually, it's all *your* fault we have to go to a party! If I hadn't found you crawling around my floor, I wouldn't have been invited any place. I could have been resting comfortably, face down in the gutter—Remember?
(JEFF *sings*)
Just in time,
I found you just in time,
Before you came, my time was running low.
I was lost,
The losing dice were tossed,
My bridges all were crossed—
No where to go.
Now you're here

And now I know just where I'm going;
No more doubt or fear—
I've found my way.
For love came just in time;
You found me just in time
And changed my lonely life that lovely day.
  (*Several people have entered and are watching with interest.*)

MAN

(*Applauding*)
Hey, you guys must be professionals.

JEFF

(*Satirically*)
Why, you rascal, you've been peeking. (*To* ELLA) Shall we do that little number we used to do in Chicago?

ELLA

Where?

JEFF

The stockyards. Are you ready, partner?

ELLA

(*Falling into the spirit of the thing*)
Let's slaughter 'em!

JEFF

(*He dances a few steps, à la Astaire-Kelly, then indicates* ELLA
with a "take-it-away" gesture)
My partner, Miss Twinkletoes Scott!

ELLA

(*Dancing toward him*)

Nothing at all!
(*She takes his hand and dances around him.*)

JEFF

Easy on the arm. It only bends one way—
(*They continue a corny little song and dance routine, made up of scraps of old vaudeville and musical movie turns.*)

BOTH

(*Facing each other*)

Tea for two and two for tea. One—two—three—four.
(JEFF *dances away from her.*)

ELLA

Where you going?

JEFF

Over here on one leg.

ELLA

Wait for me!
(*They continue dancing. As the dance reaches a "torrid" climax,* ELLA *almost delivers a "bump."*)

Hey, wait a minute! Don't give them everything.
(*Ad libs from the crowd, wanting more.* JEFF *gets down
on one knee.* ELLA *sits on his other knee.* JEFF *sings*)
Just in time

(ELLA)

Do de do do do de do

(JEFF)

I found you just in time

(ELLA)

Do de do de do de do
(*She lets her handkerchief trail over his face.*)

(JEFF)

Before you came, my time—

(ELLA)

Do do—

(JEFF)

Was running—
(ELLA, *rising and singing in a high-pitched, babyish
voice*)
This act could play the Palladium
Or even the Yankee Stadium!

(JEFF, *rising*)

I was lost

(ELLA)
He was lost

(JEFF)
The losing dice were tossed

(ELLA)
They were tossed

(JEFF)
My bridges all were crossed

(ELLA)
They were crossed

(JEFF)
No where to go
(JEFF *and* ELLA *"conduct" the assembled citizens in two
separate groups.*)

(CROWD *sings*)
Now you're here
And now I know just where I'm going;
No more doubt or fear—
I've found my way.
(JEFF *and* ELLA's *eyes meet, and they suddenly forget the
people and their vaudeville routine as they join each
other center stage and kiss tenderly.*)

(JEFF *sings*)
For love came just in time;
You found me just in time

126

(BOTH)

And changed my lonely life that lovely day.

(They stroll off slowly, arm in arm, completely wrapped up in each other, turning for just a moment to wave fondly at the people, who wave back smilingly as they disperse.)

The Lights Fade

SCENE 3

LARRY HASTINGS' *penthouse apartment. A spacious, elegant living room, chic and tastefully modern, with large French doors in back opening onto a terrace. In the background are the twinkling lights of the city at night.*

A large party is in progress—the men in evening clothes and the women in elegant sheaths, mainly of pastel shades.

As the curtain rises, the guests are grouped around the piano, applauding some smart bit of patter, no doubt. JEFF *and* ELLA *enter happily. Several people turn to greet them.* ELLA's *vivid red ball gown creates a rather "fish-out-of-water" contrast to the modern elegance of the assembled ladies. The guests ad-lib greetings.*

JEFF

Hey, listen, everyone. This is Melisande Scott. Mr. and Mrs. Trent, Lenny Wendell, Dan Zachary, Mr. and Mrs. Courtney, Veronica Smith, and—

(ELLA *is saying how-do-you-do's, very much aware of how the girls are dressed and feeling them sizing her up.*)

PAUL ARNOLD
(*A tall, good-looking chap*)

Hello, Jeff!

JEFF

Paul Arnold! Paul, this is Melisande Scott.

128

PAUL

How do you do.

ELLA

How do you do. I've admired your work in the movies—

PAUL

Thank you, dear. (*To* JEFF) Listen, I read the script. I agree with Larry. I think it's coming along swell.

JEFF

Thanks, Paul.

PAUL

And we both liked that kid we auditioned today—Blake Barton. Okay to sign him for the part of the young dentist?

JEFF

Blake Barton? Sure.
(ELLA *perks up happily upon hearing this bit of informa-tion.*)

PAUL

Miss Scott, I hope you won't think I'm rude, but I've got to drag Jeff off for about five minutes—a business talk with **Larry.**

JEFF

I was afraid something like this would happen. (*He looks around and spots a friend*) Oh, Michelle!

MICHELLE

(*A very,* very *chic and poised young lady*)
Jeff, darling!

129

JEFF

Michelle, will you look after Mel? She doesn't know the gang yet.

MICHELLE
(*Looking her over*)

I'd be delighted.

JEFF
(*To* ELLA)

Five minutes—that's all.

ELLA
(*Bravely*)

Oh, sure. I'll be fine.
(JEFF *and* PAUL *exit.*)

MICHELLE

Oh, what a pity, darling. You just missed seeing Josh!

ELLA

Ohhhhhh. Josh who?

MICHELLE

Josh Logan!

ELLA
(*Dubiously*)

Oh.
(*A small group passes by, talking animatedly*)

MAN

I tell you it was dear diary night. Mary and Ethel sang for

130

hours around the fireplace—(*To* ELLA, *who has, somehow, joined them*) Oh, hello.

ELLA

Hello. Mary and Ethel who?

MAN

Mary Martin and Ethel Merman.

ELLA

(*Feeling idiotic*)

Oh.
 (*Another group drifts by.*)

ANOTHER MAN

Well, it was a pretty memorable gathering. All those wonderful people who'd been in the Theatre fifty years or more— Mary and Ethel and—

ELLA

(*Eagerly, with great confidence*)

Mary Martin and Ethel Merman!

MAN

No. Mary Pickford and Ethel Barrymore.

ELLA

(*Really confused*)

Oh.

BUTLER

(*He has been watching and notes* ELLA's *acute discomfort*)

Don't be flustered, miss. Do what the others do. Just drop a name.

*(The following names are tossed out in rapid succession
by the group, and a number develops between* ELLA *and
the other guests—a sort of ritual, in which* ELLA *is the
discordant note)*

Ed!

Murrow!

Noel!

Coward!

Humphrey!

Bogart!

Bennett!

Cerf!

Somerset!

Maugham!

Jennifer!

Jones!

José Ferrer and Janet Blair and Fred Astaire and Vincent
    Minelli

Daniel Mann and Lynn Fontanne, Elia Kazan, the former
    Grace Kelly

Louis Shurr and Courtney Burr and Irving Lazar

Anthony Quinn—

    (ELLA, *triumphantly*)

And Rin-Tin-Tin!

    (ALL)

Doris Day and Barry Gray and Edna Best

Arthur Loew and Vaughn Monroe, Rebecca West

Irwin Shaw and Evelyn Waugh, Errol Flynn

Rory Calhoun—

(ELLA)

And Rin-Tin-Toon!

(ALL)

Barney Baruch and King Farouk, Alistair Cooke and Debbie
and Eddie
Lucille Ball and Lauren Bacall, Hedy Lamarr, Roz Russell
and Freddie
Carol Reed and Sammy Snead and Deborah Kerr
Anna May Wong

(ELLA)

And Rong-Tong-Tong!

(MAN)

Luncheon was fun at Twenty One,
Then I had to run for drinks at the Plaza.

(GIRL)

Dined with Jean, Le Pavillon,
Then flew right on to St. Marks Piazza.

(SECOND MAN)

Took a group for onion soup at dawn to Les Halles—
It never shuts—

(ELLA)

Like Chock-Full-O'-Nuts!

(GIRL)

My Christian Dior I wore then tore,
Got fitted for a new Balenciaga.
Then to Jacques Fath for just one hat—
Got something that will drive you ga-ga—

(SECOND GIRL)

Valentina's where I've been; I just adore Val—

(THIRD GIRL)

Things with *good* lines—

(ELLA)

Like things from Klein's!
(*There is a shocked silence, then* ELLA *continues grandly*)
I do all my shopping there with Mary and Ethel.

(THIRD GIRL)

Mary and Ethel who?

(ELLA, *very flatly*)

Mary Schwartz and Ethel Hotchkiss.

(ALL)

Errol Flynn!

(ELLA)

Rin-Tin-Tin!

(ALL)

Edmund Gwenn!

(ELLA)

Ren-Ten-Ten!

(ALL)

Ali Khan!

(ELLA)

Rahn-Tahn-Tahn!

(ALL)

Raymond Massey!

(ELLA, *almost stopped, but coming through*)

Lassie!

(ALL)

THAT'S the way you play the game.

Drop that name!

(ELLA, *slightly stunned by her ordeal stands with her hand extended over her head in the last gesture of the number, until the group has drifted away into groups of threes and fours. She lowers her hands as* JEFF *enters.*)

JEFF

Mel!

ELLA

(*With hysterical alacrity*)

Mel Ferrer!

JEFF

Are you all right?

ELLA

(*Taking his arm*)

Oh—yes—

JEFF

Sorry I took so long, darling—but, as a matter of fact, I spent most of the time talking about you.

ELLA

About me?

135

JEFF

And this is *the* Larry Hastings.

ELLA

(*Highly interested. It is another subscriber*)
So you're Larry Hastings!

LARRY

So you're the wonder girl!

ELLA

(*A little uneasy*)
Jeff, what did you say about me?

LARRY

Listen, if one-tenth of what this maniac says about you is
true, you're fantastic! How did you do it? He claims you're
the most brilliant woman since Madame Curie, and when I
see the change in Jeff I think you're the greatest magician since
Houdini! Thank you.
(*The guests begin crowding around her and, during the
following,* ELLA *progresses from uneasiness to discomfort
to embarrassed despair.*)

MICHELLE

My dear, I hear that you can tell all about people the second
you meet them. It's spooky!

PAUL

(*Entering*)
Hey, Miss Scott, I've got to get a better look at you! Jeff's
been singing your praises. From his description, I pictured you

in a turban with a crystal ball. He said you have the most fabulous intuition, the greatest intelligence, the deepest understanding and insight—

JEFF

(*Putting his arm around* ELLA)
It's all true—and not only that, she's a great deal prettier than Sigmund Freud.

MICHELLE

May I come around some time for a character reading?

MAN

Show us how you do it, Miss Scott. Do we have to turn out the lights and all hold hands or what?

WOMAN

Oh, I just love séances. Is that what she does?

JEFF

(*Sensing that she is highly uncomfortable*)
Oh, come on, gang—that's enough.

LARRY

Let's all have some supper. Jeff, bring Miss Scott and come along—
(*All start toward the terrace.*)

ELLA

(*Holding back, tensely*)
Jeff.

137

JEFF

(*To others*)

We'll be with you in a minute.

ELLA

(*Desperately*)

Jeff, I want to talk to you. All those things you told them about me. I'm not really like that. I'm nothing like that.

JEFF

What are you talking about? You're wonderful!

ELLA

But you said I had "the most fabulous intuition," "the deepest insight"— I—

JEFF

Well, it's true. You do—

ELLA

(*Searching for the right words*)

But, Jeff—suppose I didn't? Suppose I really weren't like that at all? Would it matter a lot to you? I mean, how would you feel about me? I mean suppose—

JEFF

What's all this supposing? That's what you are. That's why I fell in love with you. (ELLA *crumples visibly. He senses something is wrong*) Look—let's cut out of here. I'll say good night to Larry.

(*He exits to terrace.* ELLA *looks after him. She is now standing alone.*)

THE BELLS ARE RINGING

(ELLA *sings with a sort of trancelike resignation*)
He's in love with Melisande Scott,
A girl who doesn't exist.
He's in love with someone you're not,
And so, remember, it was never you he kissed.

The party's over—
It's time to call it a day—
No matter how you pretend
You knew it would end this way.
It's time to wind up the masquerade—
Just make your mind up—
The piper must be paid.
The party's over—
The candles flicker and dim—
You danced and dreamed through the night—
It seemed to be right, just being with him.
Now you must wake up—
All dreams must end—
Take off your make-up—
The party's over—
It's all over, my friend.

(*With sad determination, she hurriedly writes a note to*
JEFF, *leaves it on the couch and exits as*

The Curtains Close

SCENE 4

Crying Gypsy Café. An East Side, sort of Yorkville–Mittel-Europa spot with a seedy mural depicting Emperor Franz Joseph surrounded by assorted dancing Bavarian natives in Tyrolean garb.

SUE *is seated at a table;* SANDOR *is pacing hysterically; and the two Corvello* HENCHMEN *stand nearby—calm but menacing.*

SANDOR

But—it's impossible! A wrong order! Impossible! I must think—!

SUE

Sandor, who are those gentlemen?

SANDOR

(*Wryly*)

Two musicians from the Chicago Symphony Orchestra.

HENCHMAN

Look, Sandor—you switched the orders. We're stuck with the wrong shipment, and Maestro Corvello says you'll have to cover the cost to the tune of five thousand, six hundred albums.

SANDOR

Five thousand, six hundred albums! Gentlemen! I am inno-
cent—and I refuse!

HENCHMAN

Well, in that case, Sandor, we may find it necessary to take
you across the river for a recording session.

SANDOR

A recording session—?!

HENCHMAN

Yes. Maestro Corvello is waiting to record Siegfried's Rhine
Journey and Funeral March.
(SANDOR *groans.*)

SUE

(*Sweetly*)

Sandor, don't let little business worries upset you. You'll get
ulcers.

HENCHMAN

Yeah. Perforated ulcers! We'll be back. You got two hours.
(*They exit.*)

SUE

'Bye, 'bye! (SANDOR *groans and sits heavily, his face buried in
his hands*) You've just got to learn to relax! You know, you
need someone to look after you and keep you from driving
yourself— Well—a woman.

SANDOR

(*He leaps up and kneels beside her, taking her hand*)
Sue—your saying so sweet thoughts makes it possible for me

to speak. You see, Titanic Records is now affiliated with one of the biggest rackets—*record* combines—my English!—which in turn means more eventual expansion for Susanswerphone. (*He is quite beside himself*) Sue—how much money have you got?? You must trust me. I am talking to you as someone who *may* love you—

(*He kisses her hand.*)

SUE

I have about sixty-five hundred dollars. It's at my apartment in a little blue sock.

SANDOR

(*Simply*)

Sue, I love you.

(SUE *sings, ecstatically*)
You said it! You said it!
I heard you say it! Oh, Sandor!

(SANDOR, *with gypsy passion*)
Sue, Sue, Sue, I love you honey.
Sue, Sue, Sue, give me your money.
With your life savings in the little blue sock—

(SUE)
We will have enough to keep us out of hock—

(SANDOR)
We'll fly together to a place I know
Where we oh so happy will be.

(SUE)
Oh, where, oh, where is this place of mystery?

(SANDOR)

Where? Oh—
  (*Improvising quickly*)
In Salzburg by the sea
Where love and laughter live eternally!
In Salzburg by the hill
Where gondolas go gliding by the mill!

(SUE)

What a thrill, darling!

(SANDOR)

Tropical nights!

(SUE)

Festival lights!

(SANDOR)

Strudel for two at the midnight bullfights!
  (*He spins her.*)

(SUE, *in mad abandonment*)
Arriba!

(SANDOR)

In Salzburg, lovely Salzburg
Where the flying fishes play—
Where the schnitzel is high as an elephant's eye
And the skies are not cloudy all day—
Come to Salzburg with me—*Liebchen!* By the sea. *Olé!*
  (*He starts dragging her off stage*)
Come on, Sue.

SUE

(Thrilled and delighted)

Oh, Sandor, tell me more!

SANDOR

You want more?

(Looks at watch, mops his brow and then reluctantly continues)

In Salzburg by the sea

Where all the world's in love with gay Paree!

(SUE)

You said you love me!

(SANDOR)

In Salzburg on the shore—

(SUE)

He loves me!

(SANDOR)

Where Geisha girls keep coming back for more.

(SUE)

Sandor!

(SANDOR)

Liebchen!

(SUE)

We'll live in style—

(SANDOR)

Gold by the pile—

(BOTH)

Goulash for two as we barge down the Nile!
In Salzburg, lovely Salzburg—

(SANDOR)

Where the corn and 'taters grow!

(SUE)

In our sweet home sweet home
All the roads lead to Rome—

(SANDOR)

So, my darling, let's hurry and go!

(BOTH)

Come to Salzburg with me—*Liebchen!* By the sea! *Olé!*
(*He finally manages to get her off.*)

Curtain

SCENE 5

The Pyramid Club. A lush, gaudy café executed in the style of an Egyptian sarcophagus. It is hideous. JEFF *and* LARRY *are at a table near the bar.* JEFF *is in a state of total dejection.*

LARRY

(*Rising*)

Jeff, it's no use. We've covered every place in town. Come on back to the party.

JEFF

She and I had a plan to go dancing here. I don't know the first thing about her—where she lives—how to reach her—

LARRY

Jeff, let's go—

JEFF

No. Larry—and don't worry about *The Midas Touch*. I'll keep working.

LARRY

Good.

> (LARRY *exits.* BLAKE BARTON, *the actor, now conservatively dressed in Brooks Brothers style, enters and goes to the bar.*)

146

BARTON

Hey, daddio—gimme a double Old Rarity on the rocks. (*He spots* JEFF *and comes over to the table*) Say, Mr. Moss—

JEFF

Yeah?

BARTON

(*Eagerly*)

Don't you know me? I'm Blake Barton. Gee, I love the part they set me for in your play today. You know—this young dentist—wantsa be a composer. It's a very interesting part. Where do you writers get an idea like that from? I mean where do you get 'em from?

JEFF

(*With sudden fury*)

Aah, shut up, will ya!

BARTON

(*Offended, starting to leave*)

Excuse me, Mr. Moss.

JEFF

(*Grabbing his arm, very sorry*)

I'm sorry, Barton. I—uh—I feel rotten. Well, let's put it this way—I wish I were dead.

BARTON

(*Seating himself*)

Gee, Mr. Moss—I know how you feel. A couple of weeks ago I was lower than a duck's behind—hadn't worked in months— then, a miracle happened.

JEFF

Please—no miracles. I've got miracles of my own to worry about.

(FRANCIS *and* BARNES *have appeared on the other side of the club.*)

BARNES

(*Seeing* JEFF *and* BARTON)

There's two of her sidekicks now. The third one must be around here some place. Francis, we're going to close in tonight.

FRANCIS

Are you sure?

BARNES

Positive. No one but me knows she's Miss Big. It's a ring of counterfeiters. Come on.

(*They duck off as fanfare sounds and the* MASTER OF CEREMONIES *enters and dashes to the center of the dance floor.*)

MASTER OF CEREMONIES

And now folks, the Pyramid Club presents its new all-summer review, featuring music and lyrics by Joe Kitchell!

(*Four* DANCING GIRLS *enter, dressed in brief attire. A corny number ensues, made up of all the bits we have heard* DR. KITCHELL *composing on the air hose in his office. The number is about on a par with the general decor of the club.*)

(GIRLS *sing, in terrible voices*)

Oh,

First you're hot and then you're cold,

Then you're shy and then you're bold,
But I'm always sensitive to you.
First you fill my heart with pain,
Then your kiss is novacaine,
But I'm always sensitive to you—
> (*As the* GIRLS *exit an Elvis Presley-type* SINGER *comes to the microphone and sings as an adagio team performs, with the girl being hurled about in the customary fashion.*)

> (SINGER)

You don't see anything—
But it hurts!
'Though you can't see the pain in my heart!
Oh—oh—how it hurts!
> (*Adagio dancers exit as four dancing boys in gold jackets enter and sing and dance in rock-and-roll fashion.*)

> (BOYS *sing*)

The Midas Touch, the mighty, mighty, mighty, mighty
  Midas Touch!
The Midas Touch, the mighty, mighty, mighty, mighty
  Midas Touch!
The Midas Touch! The mighty, mighty, Midas Touch!
Gold in the morning; gold in the evening;
Gold in the summer; gold in the winter.
> (DANCING GIRLS *return in abbreviated gold costumes.*)

> (GIRLS)

Dr. Midas said to me,
"Be sure you take your vitamins G-O-L-D."

And that's what he said to me.
Hey!

(*As the* BOYS *and* GIRLS *dance, they scatter great handfuls
of gold dust on themselves and the customers. The Elvis
Presley* SINGER *returns to conclude the number with the
microphone turned up to a deafeningly loud pitch.*)

(SINGER)

Gold in all it's glory—
And that's the story—
Of the Midas Touch!

(*As all the performers take their final tableau, a mighty
shower of gold dust is released upon them from above.
During the "Midas Touch" portion of the number,* JEFF
*has been listening in growing bewilderment. As the
applause dies down,* DR. KITCHELL, *now in street clothes,
can be seen walking up and down among the tables in
a state of happy excitement.*)

KITCHELL

(*Applauding*)

Wonderful, Wonderful—I wrote those songs. Great, wasn't
it? I wrote those songs!

JEFF

(*Stopping him*)

You wrote that *last* song? "The Midas Touch"?

KITCHELL

Yeah. Great title, isn't it?

JEFF

I always thought so. Won't you join us?

KITCHELL

(*Sitting, very pleased*)

Thanks. My name is Joe Kitchell.

JEFF

How do you do. Jeffrey Moss. Blake Barton. (*They shake hands*) Tell me, Mr. Kitchell—

KITCHELL

It's *Dr.* Kitchell. Actually, I'm a dentist.

JEFF

A dentist?!

BARTON

A dentist?!

KITCHELL

Sure.

BARTON

That's *funny*. I'm a *dentist*.

KITCHELL

You're a dentist?

BARTON

No, I mean, I play a dentist in a play.

KITCHELL

(*Rather surprised*)

That's funny. Well, I'm not a dentist any more. I'm a composer now. My father didn't want me to be a composer, but—

BARTON

(*Disbelieving*)

My father doesn't want *me* to be a composer—

KITCHELL

He doesn't?

BARTON

My father in the play.

KITCHELL

(*A little staggered*)

That's funny.

BARTON

Very interesting part. Real funny and sad. You know—I make up these tunes on the air hose.

KITCHELL

(*Totally stunned*)

I wrote "The Midas Touch" on the air hose.

JEFF

(*Who has been listening in quiet amazement*)

So that's what's holding up the play. I was using paper.

152

KITCHELL

What play?

BARTON

The play we're talking about. He wrote it.

KITCHELL
(*To* JEFF)

You wrote the play?

JEFF

Yeah. It's called *The Midas Touch*.

KITCHELL
(*Filled with awe in the presence of the occult*)
That's the name of my song!

JEFF

Yeah, I know.

ALL THREE

That's funny.
(*They all stare at each other with wild surmise. They
think they are going mad. Complete silence.*)

KITCHELL

Oh, I remember now—I got that title from that girl.

JEFF

What girl?

153

KITCHELL

The girl that said she was thinking of the "Midas Touch" that day.

JEFF

What day?

KITCHELL

Oh, the day that changed my whole life. I was feeling lower than low—hopeless—and suddenly a miracle happened.

JEFF

A miracle?

BARTON

He's got a miracle, too.

KITCHELL

This girl—she wasn't in the office more than a coupla minutes—tipped me off on this job—and I got it. She was blond, pretty, about five-feet-six, big brown eyes—

JEFF *and* BARTON
(*Both grab* KITCHELL)

Wait! Wait a second!

BARTON

Listen, Mr. Moss, that's how I got the chance at the part in your play! Some girl comes up to me in the drug store. She tipped me off about myself. I get the part. She changed my life! What I'm working up to is—she's blond, five-feet-six, pretty, big brown eyes—

154

JEFF

(Leaping up, wild eyed)

Melisande!

BARTON *and* KITCHELL

Who?

JEFF

Melisande Scott! Where is she?

BARTON

(Rushing off, followed by KITCHELL*)*

He's flippin'! Let's get outta here!

JEFF

(Catching them)

No—no— Wait! This girl you're talking about is the same girl who dropped into my life.

KITCHELL

(Befuddled)

Same girl?

JEFF

Yeah. When did you see her last?

KITCHELL

She was in the office a coupla minutes and disappeared. I never saw her again.

BARTON

Same with me.

JEFF

(*Highly excited*)

Look, you guys—I'm going to get to the bottom of this. I've got to find her. I'm in love with her! Where can I call you later?

BARTON

I don't know where I'll be.

KITCHELL

I don't know where I am.

BARTON

(*Writing on match cover*)

Look—I'll give you my phone number.

KITCHELL

(*Taking card from his pocket*)

I'll give you my phone number, too.

JEFF

Thanks!

(*He takes the matches and card and starts off.*)

BARTON

Where ya goin'?

JEFF

Bay Ridge!

(*He is gone.*)

BARTON

Good luck! Bay Ridge. Seems like a logical move.

KITCHELL

When in doubt, I *always* go to Bay Ridge.
  (BARNES, FRANCIS *and the cops enter.*)

BARNES

Okay, you two! Come along.
  (KITCHELL *and* BARTON *are grabbed in viselike grips by
  a cop.*)

KITCHELL

Wait a minute! What *is* this?

BARNES

You're coming to the station for some questioning.

BARTON

Would this have anything to do with a blond girl?

BARNES
  (*With big grin*)

You said it!

KITCHELL *and* BARTON

That's funny!
  (*The cops start to pull them off.*)

KITCHELL

Wait!
  (*They stop. He starts to sing*)

THE BELLS ARE RINGING

That's funny—that you love me like you do!
    (The cops pull them off as he continues to sing.)

Quick Curtain

Scene 6

A subway platform. A sign reads Bay Ridge. A MAN *is in the phone booth.* JEFF *is frantically looking through the phone directory. The* MAN *comes out of the booth.*

JEFF

Excuse me—Do you know anybody around here named Melisande Scott?

MAN

You must be from out of town.
(*He exits.* JEFF *throws down the phone book and stands, discouraged, thinking of* ELLA.)

(JEFF *sings, sadly, to himself*)
I pictured someone who'd walk and talk and smile as you
    do—
Who'd make me feel as you do right now!
But that was long before I held you,
Long before I kissed you,
Long before I touched you and felt this glow;
But now you really are here and now at last I know
That long before I knew you, I loved you so.
(*He stands there a moment, defeated. Then*)
Kitchell.
(*He takes the card from his pocket, enters the phone booth and dials the number on it.*)

SUE'S VOICE

Dr. Kitchell's Dental Clinic.

JEFF

Where can I reach the doctor?

SUE'S VOICE

Dr. Kitchell left no message.

JEFF

Is this—Susanswerphone?

SUE'S VOICE

That is correct. Who's calling?

JEFF

Never mind. (*He hangs up, puzzled*) Susanswerphone.
(*He takes out the match cover and dials.*)

SUE'S VOICE

Blake Barton's residence.

JEFF

(*More puzzled*)

Susanswerphone?

SUE'S VOICE

Yes . . .
(JEFF *hangs up, steps out of the booth.*)

JEFF

(*Now extremely puzzled*)

That's funny. Kitchell, Barton and me—all Susanswerphone.
That was the other one I talked to—Mom—Melisande—(*A
look of dawning realization comes over his face. Then, in-*

credulously, softly) Mom? *(Louder, convinced, Eureka-time)*
Mom! *(Then, yelling as if the sound could reach all the way to
New York)* M—O—O—O—M!!!!
   (He dashes off.)

Quick Curtain

SCENE 7

Susanswerphone. SUE *is at the switchboard, looking troubled.*
ELLA, *in street clothes, is finishing packing a suitcase, collecting belongings around the place.*

SUE

Well, I admit what you did *was* kind of extreme—but I know you were only trying to help. Please don't go, Ella.

ELLA

I have to, Sue. I couldn't bear to hear his voice day after day.

SUE

Ella, if you feel the way you do about him, you should tell him.

ELLA

Oh, Sue, I can't. I don't want him to know it was all a trick. I've been walking and thinking for hours, and suddenly it hit me. I'm not real. I've spent half my life tuning in on other people's lives, playing all kinds of imaginary characters—even with someone I fell in love with—and when the make-believe love became *real,* it had no place to go—because *I* wasn't real. Actually, it's what you've been telling me all along. I don't really know my subscribers—they don't really care about me.

THE BELLS ARE RINGING

SUE

That's not true! Only today Mrs. Mallet called twice about her little son, Junior. He wanted to talk to Santa Claus. They always ask for you. They call me the *other* one.

ELLA

The trouble is, I don't really know myself who I am.
(*She sings*)
I know you; your name is Sue.
But who am I?
I've gotta find out.
At least—I'm gonna try.

I'm going back
Where I can be me—
At the Bonjour Tristesse Brassière Company—
They've got a great big switchboard there
Where it's just "hello—good-bye—"
It may be dull, but there I can be
Just me, myself and I—
A little modeling on the side—
Yes, that's where I'll be—
At the Bonjour Tristesse Brassière Company—
And if anybody asks for Ella, Mella or Mom
Tell them that I'm going back where I came from—
To the B. T. Brassière Company—

(*With exaggerated "blues" mannerisms*)
Good-bye, everybody—Good-bye, Madame Grimaldi—
Good-bye, Junior Mallet—Santa Claus is hittin' the road—
Listen to your mama, mama, mama—

Eat your spinach, baby—Eat your spinach, baby, by the load—

(*Changing to French chanteuse style*)
La Petite Bergère Restaurant—*adieu,*
Je ne reviendrai jamais—jamais—jamais
C'est tous fini— Adieu— to you—
So Good-bye, Max, and your dogs and your cats—
To the Duke of Windsor and his Duchess—
Good-bye, Barton, Kitchell and Hastings—
At last you're out of my clutches.
I'll miss you, but you'll carry on—
You'll never know that I've gone—

(*In all-out "Mammy" style*)
I'm going back
Where I can be me—
To the Bonjour Tristesse Brassière Company—
And while I'm sitting there, I hope that I'll find out
Just what Ella Peterson is all about
In that Shangri-la of lacy lingerie—
A little modeling on the side—
At the Bonjour Tristesse Brassière Company—

Send me my mail there!
To the Bonjour Tristesse Brassière Company.
(*She exits with her suitcase but returns immediately*)
I forgot my canary.
(SANDOR *enters, followed by the two* CORVELLO HENCH-MEN.)

HENCHMAN

Come on, Sandor! The money!

SANDOR

(*Going to his books checking the accounts*)

In a minute! But first I must find out who changed those orders for Beethoven's Tenth to Beethoven's Ninth? Who could have done that?

ELLA

Oh, I did. You know, Beethoven only wrote nine symphonies.

SANDOR

(*Exploding*)

You idiot! You put all the money on the wrong horse! I was almost bumped off for this by the Corvello mob!

HENCHMAN

Shut up!

SANDOR

To think my simple little bookie system could be loused up by this dumb broad!

ELLA

Horses!

SUE

Bookies! Sandor—is *that* what I gave you all that money for?

ELLA

Sue, you didn't!

HENCHMAN

That's swell, loud mouth! Now these dames know all about it!

SANDOR

What's the difference! They can't talk! They're as much in this as we are. One peep out of them and the cops put them in jail and close up Susanswerphone!

SUE

Oh, no!

HENCHMAN

The money! Let's go!

SUE

My life savings! Ella, please!

HENCHMAN

Shut up!

ELLA
(*Laughs wildly*)

They don't get it!

SUE

Get what?

ELLA
(*To* SUE, *picking up the exact tone and manner of the* HENCHMAN)

Shut up! (*To* SANDOR) Inspector Barnes!

SANDOR

Barnes?

ELLA

Barnz! B-A-R-N-Z!

SANDOR

Z?

ELLA

Z!! The whole thing was a trap. He was after you the whole time!

SANDOR

But—it's impossible!

HENCHMAN

(*Grabbing girls*)

Then you're both coming—to Corvello's!

ELLA

(*Laughs again, improvising rapidly*)

It won't do any good to rub us out, because—because you've all been spillin' your guts into a tape recorder!

MEN

Where is it?!

ELLA

Where is it? Think you're playing with kids? Where is it! Where is it?? Why, it's hooked up to the police station! As a matter of fact, Barnes should be here any minute!

BARNES

(*Entering, followed by a policeman. FRANCIS and another police-man enter from the door stage right*)

Awright!!

THE BELLS ARE RINGING

ELLA

(Screams)

Ohhh! Inspector Barnes! Am I glad to see you!

(She falls against him, relieved.)

BARNES

All right, Miss Peterson. Get your toothbrush. Come along.

ELLA

My toothbrush? Ohh, Inspector, we can drop the act now. I've got the whole bookie ring here. Just take 'em away!

SANDOR

(Running to BARNES*)*

Inspector Barnes—I surrender happily! These are two of Corvello's henchmen!

BARNES

Huh?!

SANDOR

I want to congratulate you for having such a brilliant ally— *(Cowering behind* ELLA*)* working with you to uncover the Corvello gang! Me—I am nothing! Small potatoes! Corvello's the head of everything! We only work for him!

BARNES

(Flabbergasted)

What!

ELLA

Inspector Barnes—don't you get the picture?!! Titanic Records is a bookie operation. Take 'em away.

BARNES

(*Befuddled*)

Take 'em away!
(*The cops remove the men.* SANDOR *hangs back.* FRANCIS *beckons.*)

SANDOR

(*To* SUE, *as he goes*)

Farewell, my *Liebchen!*

SUE

Oh, Sandor!

SANDOR

We could have made beautiful music together. (*He tosses her the blue sock containing her money*) *Aufwiedersehen!*

FRANCIS

You'll get a promotion for this, Inspector Barnes!

BARNES

But I didn't *do* anything.

FRANCIS

I told you she was a nice girl.
(*He waves his fingers to* ELLA *and exits.*)

BARNES

(*Warmly*)

Is it a crime for a man to have made a human mistake? I

169

misjudged you. (*He and* ELLA *shake hands; he starts out, then comes back, as though suddenly remembering something*) You know, those two kids might have been alive today. (*To* SUE) Would you come to the station with me? I might need your help.

SUE

I'll be glad to. Now, Ella, promise you won't leave.

ELLA

I'll watch the board till you get back.
(*Ring.*)

SUE
(*Plugs in*)
I'll take it. Susanswerphone. What? . . . Who? . . . Talk slower . . . Nobody by that name here . . . Well, it won't do you any good; there's nobody here by that name.

ELLA
(*Wearily*)
Hang up on him!

SUE
(*Unplugs*)
Crackpot!

BARNES

Come along, please.
(BARNES *exits;* SUE *starts to follow.*)

ELLA

(*In sudden panic*)

Sue! What was that?

SUE

Somebody looking for somebody. I said there was nobody here by that name.

ELLA

By what name?

SUE

Melanie or Melisande. Said he was coming down here.

ELLA

(*Terrified*)

No! Sue! I can't stay here!

SUE

Watch the board!
(*She is gone.*)

ELLA

(*Phone buzzes*)

Oh, no! I can't stay here! (*Starts out with the bird cage and her suitcase as the ringing continues. She plugs in and speaks hastily*) Max's Dog and Cat Beauty Shop. Nobody home!
(*She unplugs the connection and starts to dash out as* JEFF's VOICE *suddenly sounds off stage.*)

JEFF'S VOICE

Keep the change.

ELLA

(*In tremendous hysteria, weeping*)

Oh, no!

JEFF'S VOICE

Is Susanswerphone in this block?

CARL'S VOICE

Right here.

JEFF'S VOICE

No, no. It must be an office building.

CARL'S VOICE

This is it.

JEFF'S VOICE

Are you sure?

CARL'S VOICE

Yes.

JEFF'S VOICE

Thanks. (*During this,* ELLA *has rapidly picked up the afghan from the back of the armchair, has flung it about her shoulders, detached a mop and placed it on her head, and has found a pair of* SANDOR's *glasses and put them on. She can hardly see. She staggers to the switchboard, an insane sight, and sits hunched over like an old woman.* JEFF *enters excitedly, then stares around the office in amazement*) Hey, what kind of place *is* this? It's right out of *Oliver Twist!* (*He sees* ELLA *and is thunderstruck at the weird sight*) What?

ELLA

(*In exaggerated toothless old lady's voice*)

Keep away, young man! You have no right to be here! Now —we girls aren't allowed to be familiar with the customers. *Get out!*

JEFF

(*Realizing it is she, but playing along with it, amused. He kneels beside her*)

Mom, don't you know me? Don't you know your li'l ol' telephonic Sonny Boy?

ELLA

(*Turns and peers at him*)

Mr. Moss—oh, yes! (*Turning away immediately*) Now, get out!! (*The mop falls off. He picks it up and gently replaces it on her head. She bursts into tears, pulls it off and leaps up*) Oh, all right! Get the picture—it's *me!*

JEFF

(*Lovingly*)

Melisande!

ELLA

(*Escaping from him*)

No—ME! ELLA—Ella Peterson! There is no Melisande. I just made her up!

JEFF

(*Following her*)

All right—Ella—Mella—Mom—whatever your name is. I love you!

ELLA

But you can't! I tricked you!

JEFF

Pretty shabby trick—saving a man's life!

ELLA

But—all that intuition stuff. I was just telling you what you told Mom. I'm nothing.

JEFF

(*Very tenderly*)

Don't you call Mom "nothing." I loved talking to her. She was warm, sympathetic, understanding, wise. I thought she was a little old lady. Isn't it a nice surprise to find out she's a beautiful blond who can cha-cha!

(*He removes her glasses.*)

ELLA

You've got to let me explain what I did to you!

JEFF

(*Taking the afghan from her shoulders*)

Never mind. I've got you pretty well figured out. I had a long trip from Bay Ridge to work on it—(ELLA *crosses to the switchboard with a moan*) Kitchell, Barton, me—(*She sits on the stool, moaning again.* JEFF *kneels beside her*) Mel—Ella—Ella! You do things like that just the way you say hello to people on the subway. You're a girl with a lot of love to give. Instead of spreading it around all over the place, give it to me. I need it. I want it.

174

(He kisses her hands. Then lifts her to her feet and places her arms about his neck. They kiss. Ring. ELLA *reaches behind her, turns off the board and goes back into the embrace,* SUE, BARNES *and* GWYNNE *enter.)*

SUE

Oh—!

ELLA

(Breaking out of the embrace and presenting JEFF*)*
Sue, this is Plaza O-double four, double three.

SUE

How do you do?

BARNES

(Shaking hands)
How are you?

GWYNNE

Hi!
*(*JEFF *acknowledges the introductions.)*

BARNES

(To ELLA*)*
And here are some people who want to see you. *(He stands at the door and announces, like a butler)* Butterfield 8–9971.
*(*KITCHELL *enters.)*

ELLA

Dr. Kitchell!

175

KITCHELL

How can I ever thank you!

ELLA

Don't thank me—

KITCHELL

(*Inspired again, singing*)
Don't thank me—but let me thank you—
(*He goes to one side, writing it on paper.*)

BARNES

Murray Hill 3-9970!
(BARTON *enters.*)

ELLA

Blake Barton!

BARTON

Listen, girl—you gave my life a crazy switcheroo.

ELLA

Cuckoo!

BARTON

Cuckoo!

BARNES

Plaza 8-4099!

176

HASTINGS

Where is that wonder girl?
*(All of the subscribers enter through all of the available
doors to greet* ELLA. *They mill about as* JEFF *and* ELLA,
oblivious to all, embrace center stage.)

Curtain

"Raves" for The Fireside Theatre

"I think the idea of the Fireside Theatre is a splendid one. It will bring Broadway to thousands who hanker to get there but don't have the means or the ability."—*Gertrude Lawrence*

"Reading good plays is a very rewarding pastime. The Fireside Theatre sounds to me like a wonderful idea that will bring new delight to thousands of people. Put me down as a subscriber."—*Roland Young*

"Your proposed plan should appeal to the many who are unable to get to the Broadway theatre as well as to those who will welcome the opportunity of reading and discussing plays they have seen and liked."—*Katharine Cornell*

"The Fireside Theatre; what an excellent idea. The words seem to me to be an invitation to read plays with imagination; and not only as literature.

"I hope this club will have a wide membership in every part of the United States and that the result will be an immensely increased interest in the drama both in the theatre and at the fireside."—*Noel Coward*

"Congratulations on your grand idea of the Fireside Theatre. As one who loves books, the theatre, and an open fire I can think of no happier venture in the publishing field."—*Ilka Chase*

"The Fireside Theatre seems to me an excellent idea. It means that the theatre will once again be able to go on the road and to places seldom visited by it now. Theatrical books can be touring companies too. There is no reason why the theatre in print should not each month win wide and devoted audiences among those who, for one reason or another, must do their theatre-going at home."—*John Mason Brown*